Excel
Basic Skills

KINDERGARTEN/
FOUNDATION
K/F
Ages
5–6

Handwriting

AF865228

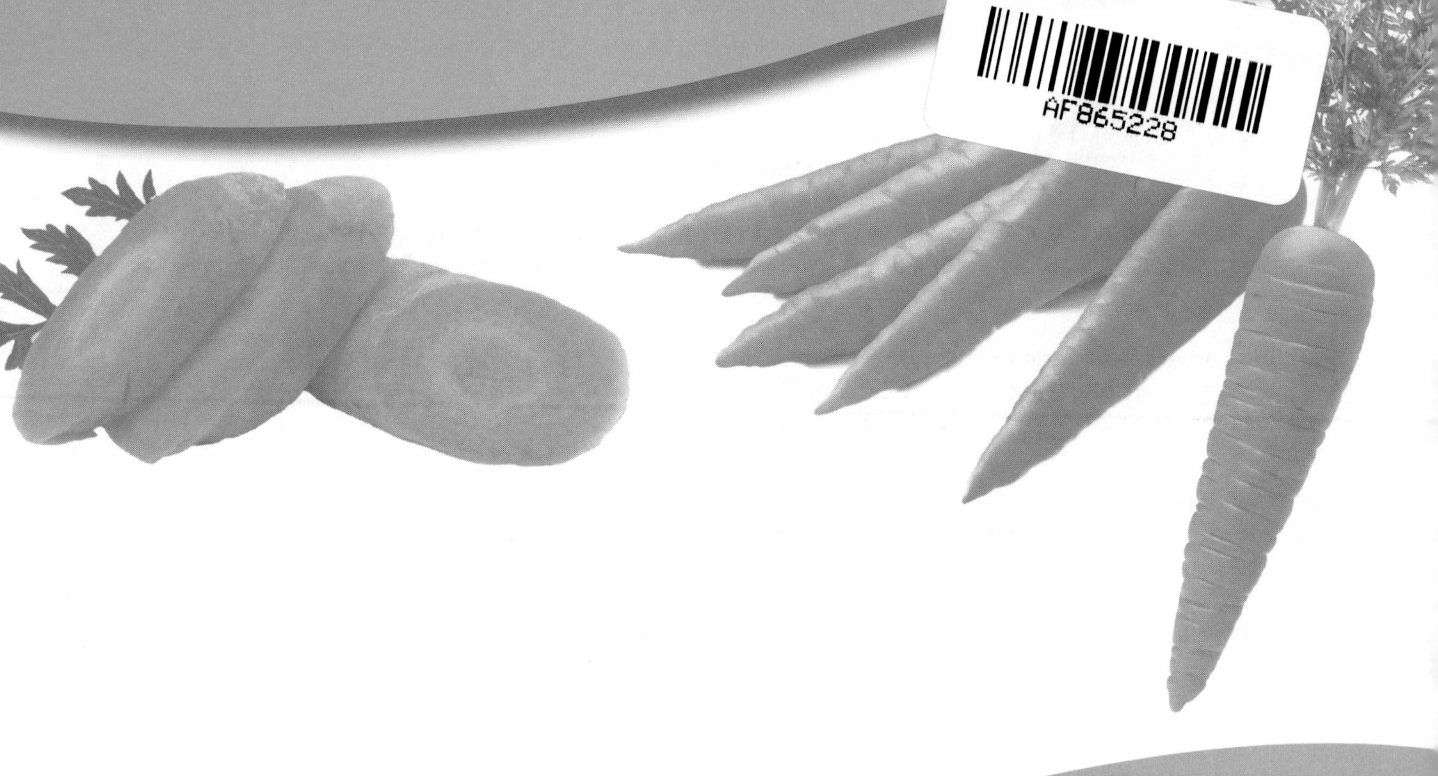

Get the Results You Want!

Ada Munro & Ivy Morgan

PASCAL
PRESS

© 2023 Ada Munro, Ivy Morgan and Pascal Press
Reprinted 2025

ISBN 978 1 74125 733 5

Pascal Press Pty Ltd
PO Box 250
Glebe NSW 2037
(02) 9198 1748
www.pascalpress.com.au

Publisher: Vivienne Joannou
Edited by Rosemary Peers
Cover and page design by Sonia Woo
Typeset by lj Design (Julianne Billington)
Printed by Vivar Printing/Green Giant Press

Reproduction and communication for educational purposes
The Australian *Copyright Act 1968* (the Act) allows a maximum of one chapter or 10% of this book, whichever is the greater, to be copied by any educational institution for its educational purposes provided that the educational institution (or the body that administers it) has given a remuneration notice to Copyright Agency under the Act.
For details of the Copyright Agency licence for educational institutions contact:

Copyright Agency
Level 12, 66 Goulburn Street
Sydney NSW 2000
Telephone: (02) 9394 7600
Facsimile: (02) 9394 7601
Email: memberservices@copyright.com.au

Reproduction and communication for other purposes
Except as permitted under the Act (for example, a fair dealing for the purposes of study, research, criticism or review) no part of this book may be reproduced, stored in a retrieval system, or transmitted in any form or by any means without prior written permission. All inquiries should be made to the publisher at the address above.

All efforts have been made to gain permission for the copyright material reproduced in this book. In the event of any oversight, the publisher welcomes any information that will enable rectification of any reference or credit in subsequent editions.

Notice of liability
The information contained in this book is distributed without warranty. While precautions have been taken in the preparation of this material, neither the authors nor Pascal Press shall have any liability to any person or entity with respect to any liability, loss or damage caused or alleged to be caused directly or indirectly by the instructions and content contained in the book.

Contents

Progress tracker

Keep track of your progress. Colour each segment as you complete the practice page.

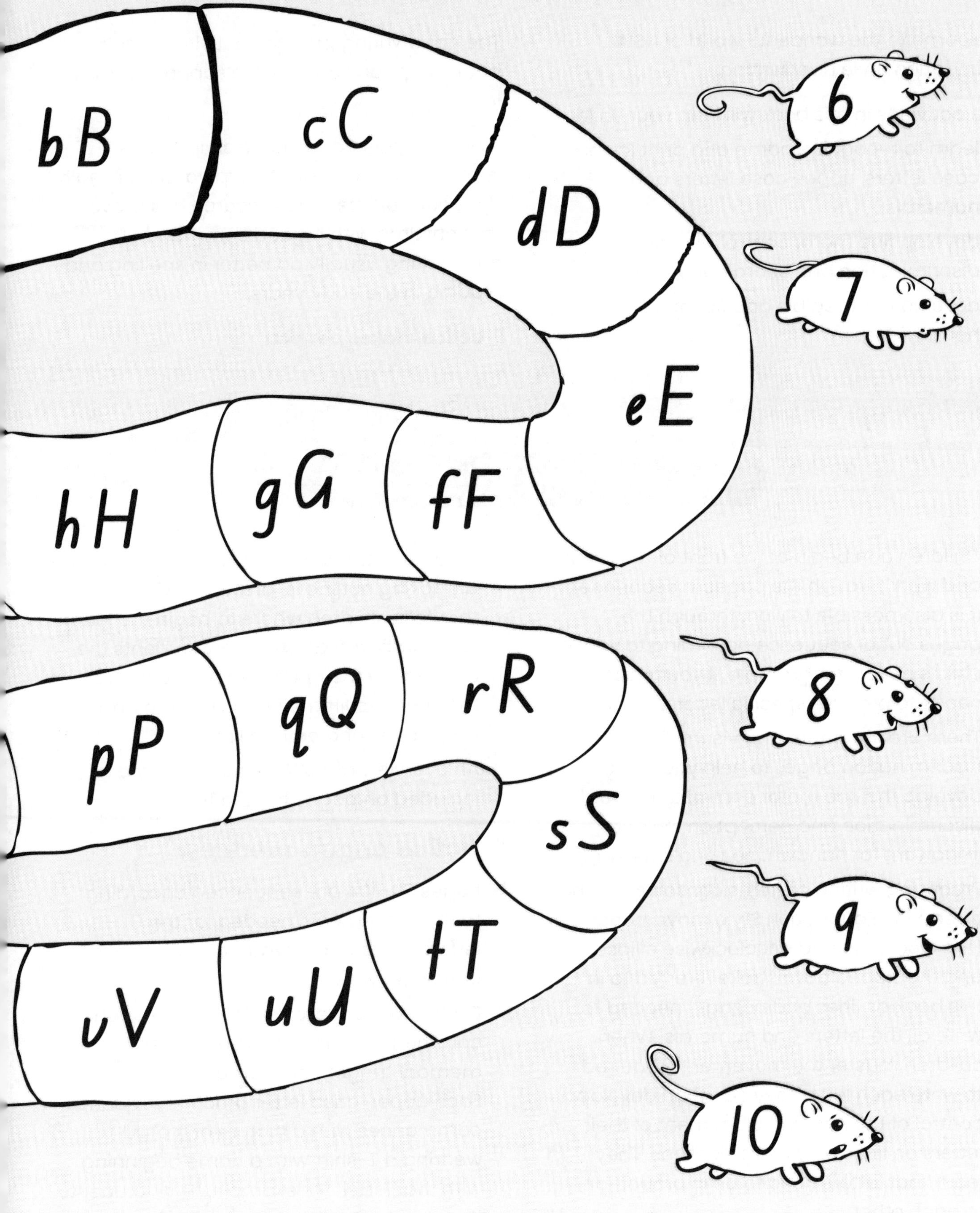
bB
cC
dD
eE
fF
gG
hH
pP
qQ
rR
sS
tT
uU
vV
6
7
8
9
10

Introduction

Welcome to the wonderful world of NSW Foundation Style handwriting.

The activities in this book will help your child:

- learn to recognise, name and print lower-case letters, upper-case letters and numerals
- develop fine motor control, visual discrimination and coordination
- develop neat, legible and fluent handwriting.

The handwriting practice activities in this book are phonics-based to support literacy learning.

A neat, legible handwriting style, where letters are of consistent shape and size, really does support literacy. Research has proven that children with a good command of handwriting usually do better in spelling and reading in the early years.

Practice makes perfect!

How to use this book

- Children can begin at the front of the book and work through the pages in sequence. It is also possible to work through the pages out of sequence according to your child's needs; for example, if your child needs to practise specific letters.
- There are 18 pattern and visual discrimination pages to help your child develop the fine motor control and visual discrimination and perception skills so important for handwriting (and spelling).
- Practising writing patterns consolidates the three NSW Foundation Style movements (the clockwise and anticlockwise ellipses and the sloped downstroke referred to in this book as lines and zigzags) needed to write all the letters and numerals. When children master the movements required to write each letter they can then develop control of the size and placement of their letters on lines or within guidelines. They learn that letters need to be in proportion to each other.
- When a letter or numeral is first introduced a tracking outline is provided, with a dot that tells children where to begin the letter. The numbered arrows show students the direction of their pencil movement and if they need to lift their pencil off the page to begin a second or third line.
- An overview of NSW Foundation Style is included on pages 110 and 111.

Practice pages overview

- Pages 30–104 are sequenced according to the movements needed for the letters (lines and zigzags, clockwise and anticlockwise).
- Each lower-case letter practice sequence commences with a phonics-based memory trigger; for example, *p* for *pig*. Each upper-case letter practice sequence commences with a picture of a child wearing a T-shirt with a name beginning with that letter; for example, *Paige*. Students then track letter movements and shapes

within an outline of the letter, trace the letter over dotted lines and then practise the letter independently with the support of a starting dot. The tracking, tracing and independent practice activities make use of the guidelines on the page. Guidelines help your child learn to write letters of consistent size relative to each other.

- The numeral practice pages start with the number of ladybirds represented by the numeral to be practised. The ladybird wings also contain a pattern of dots to help your child develop subitising. This is an important maths skill where a child can instantly recognise the number of objects in a small group, without having to count them.
- Revision pages are distributed throughout the letter and numeral pages. These pages provide further reinforcement opportunities for your child to trace the letters or numerals and to write them independently. The revision pages contain a mixture of letters and numerals.
- Every page includes a **Parent Tip** at the bottom. These contain reminders such as the need for your child to warm up their fingers and wrist; comments on aspects of the three Ps (posture, paper tilt and pencil grip); or suggestions as to what to watch for when your child is forming the letters and numerals.

Writing words

- Three pages (pages 105–107) provide the opportunity for your child to practise writing words. This allows them to practise appropriate spacing between letters within a word and also between words. The words on these pages have been chosen from the 25 most common words in English that make up about a third of all reading and writing. Your child should learn to recognise these words instantly and to write them correctly.
- Finally two pages with blank guidelines are provided on pages 108 and 109. Children can use these pages to write and practise words they need or want to use or that they use frequently. Children should be given the autonomy to write the words they choose for themselves on these pages.

Progress tracker

- The progress tracker on pages 4 and 5 is a quick reference that you can use to watch your child's progress through the letters and numerals. Your child can colour each segment or mouse that corresponds to a completed work page.

Activities to support the development of handwriting

- Fine motor skills are essential for children's independence in performing everyday tasks, such as feeding themselves, doing up buttons and zips or tying shoelaces, as well as school tasks, such as writing and cutting. Children with poor fine motor skills can struggle academically and their self-esteem can suffer too. Imagine how the child with illegible handwriting feels when they cannot read their own handwritten work.
- Watch your child as they engage in fine motor activities, such as using pegs, rolling playdough, threading, and using a knife and fork or chopsticks. How is their coordination and control?
- These activities can be done anytime with your child to help build their writing muscles.

Activities to support the development of handwriting		
Activity	**How it helps**	**What to talk about**
building with blocks	‣ fine motor control ‣ hand-eye coordination ‣ perceptual discrimination	on top of, beside, above, low, high, spatial relationships such as how each block fits within the space and in relation to other blocks
cutting	‣ fine motor control ‣ hand-eye coordination	straight, curved
drawing patterns	‣ fine motor control ‣ hand-eye coordination ‣ holding implements	sequence (between, before, after, next), oval, slope, straight, up, down, top, bottom, left, right, clockwise, anticlockwise
drawing with pencils, chalk, crayons	‣ fine motor control ‣ hand-eye coordination ‣ holding implements	size, shape, proportion, spatial relationships such as how the drawing fits within the space and in relation to other items in the drawing
drawing with water pistols on a fence or wall	‣ gross motor control ‣ hand-eye coordination	size, shape, straight, oval, top, bottom
finger painting	‣ motor control ‣ hand-eye coordination	left, right, top, bottom
jigsaws	‣ visual discrimination ‣ visual memory	spatial relationships such as how each piece relates to another, the shape of a piece and the shape of a space to fit it
mazes	‣ hand-eye coordination	start, direction, finish, left, right
measuring and pouring	‣ fine motor control ‣ hand-eye coordination ‣ manipulative skills	in, out, full, empty, about half full, about half empty, less, more
modelling in sand or playdough	‣ fine motor control ‣ manipulative skills	under, over, above, beside, size, shape
painting with a brush	‣ motor control ‣ hand-eye coordination ‣ holding implements	up, down, over, above, under
pasting	‣ fine motor control ‣ hand-eye coordination	spatial relationships such as the size and shape of the item to be pasted in relation to the space available to paste it
playing Dominoes or Snap	‣ visual discrimination	shape, same, different, matching
screwing and unscrewing	‣ fine motor control	size, shape, direction of rotation
sewing	‣ fine motor control ‣ hand-eye coordination	sequence, in, out, bottom, through, next, after
tearing and folding paper	‣ fine motor control ‣ hand-eye coordination	in, out, along, straight, beginning, end
threading	‣ fine motor control ‣ hand-eye coordination	in, on, next, before, after, size

Tips for effective handwriting

- The poster on page 112 can be used by your child as a reminder and to help them develop self-correcting skills.

The three Ps for right-handed writers

The three Ps are:

Posture

- Remind your child to sit with a straight back and both feet flat on the floor.

Paper tilt

- The writing paper should be tilted correctly with the top right up. The helper hand can hold the paper or book in place.

Pencil grip

- Reinforce a correct grip as early as possible in your child's life so that incorrect or awkward habits don't form in the first place. Tell your child to hold the pencil 2 cm from the tip between their index finger and their thumb with its shaft in the open web between index finger and thumb. The pencil rests on the middle finger. The heel of the writing hand rests on the page so the writing hand is steady.
- Your child should use large soft-leaded pencils to begin with. Make sure writing implements are not slippery as these are more difficult to grip. You could also buy a rubber grip for your child's pencil. It can be used to help your child maintain a correct grip.

The three Ps for left-handed writers

- Ten per cent of people are left-handed and more boys than girls are left-handed.
- Being left-handed does not mean your child will have messy handwriting. It just means they will have a few extra challenges to overcome because the world is largely set up for right-handed people.

Posture

- Remind your child to sit with a straight back and both feet flat on the floor.

Paper tilt

- Tilt the page left corner up and right side down so they can see the tip of the pencil and where they are writing. Tell them to use their right hand to hold the page steady. Use a start dot on the left side of the page to remind your child where to start.

Pencil grip

- Have your child hold their pencil 2 to 3 cm from the tip. This is close enough to the tip to give them good control of the pencil but far enough away from the tip that they can see their writing.
- Make sure the shaft of the pencil rests in the web of the hand between the thumb and forefinger.
- Left-handed writers have to *push* their pencil rather than *pull* their pencil, so it is more difficult. Pulling is smoother and easier than pushing. Pushing means you are more likely to tear the paper or smudge the writing.

- Tell your child not to press too hard. Buying them pencils with softer lead will also help prevent paper tearing. Softer lead allows for softer pressure and also helps avoid hand strain. Pencils with broader tips are easier than fine tips, which tend to tear the page more readily.
- Avoid marking pens with ink that stays wet because it can smudge as your child's hand moves over it as they write.
- The grip should be relaxed and not hooked or cramped. Make sure your child keeps their wrist straight. This will avoid cramping but also allow your child to see their writing. They need to keep their hand below the writing line.
- Practising on a vertical chalkboard or whiteboard can help free up arm movements.

TIP Check that your child's classroom allows for a left-hand computer mouse and left-handed scissors.

Sitting on the left

- In any situation where two children are sharing a desk or table for writing, the **left-handed child** should sit **on the left side** of the right-handed child so they don't bump arms when writing. Make sure there's space on the left to support the child's left arm.

Handwriting troubleshooting

- Handwriting is important for writing. When handwriting is slow and laboured, and when children have trouble reading their own handwriting, it leads to frustration and embarrassment at school. Children then avoid handwriting and it becomes a vicious cycle. Without practice they can't improve. Achieving success from the very beginning is important in supporting children's confidence as writers. Efficient handwriting helps students get their thoughts on to paper quickly and their creativity can flow. Most children can improve their handwriting with practice and targeted intervention but some may always struggle.
- Parents can help identify issues early on before children's self-esteem is affected to prevent the impact that poor handwriting has on other areas of learning.

IMPORTANT Do not despair if your child has poor handwriting. Your child can improve with practice. Make practice fun and rewarding and use other activities such as those listed on pages 7 and 8 to support the various other skills that are beneficial for aspects of handwriting.

Watch your child as they write

- How do they look? Comfortable or uncomfortable? Relaxed or tense?
- What are their wrists, arms, shoulders, fingers, etc. doing as they write?

Look at the writing your child is producing

- Are the letters cramped, of irregular sizes or illegible?

Talk to your child about handwriting

- Ask them how they feel about writing. Do they enjoy it or avoid it? Do they value handwriting as a skill? If they find writing difficult, does it bother them? Are they worried about their handwriting? Do they care about handwriting? Have they seen you write to understand the importance of legible handwriting?

Handwriting problems

Issue	What's needed	How to help
Speed and fluency	Too slow indicates that your child cannot write the letters without thinking; they are needing to concentrate to try to recall what they need to do.	Your child needs to develop automaticity (where writing letters becomes automatic and they don't have to think about it).
Letter shapes and legibility	Muscle memory and automaticity	Practise movements and the shapes.
	Knowledge of where letters start and end and that letters in words are of uniform size; and that words need to be planned and their lengths estimated so they don't run into each other or run off the end of the line	Practise identifying letters, their differences and similarities.
	Knowledge that spaces exist between words and that print in English moves from left to right	Practise.
Mixing upper-case and lower-case letters	This is normal and just takes practice. Developing awareness and visual discrimination will lead to your child learning to recognise the differences.	Do activities to develop visual discrimination (see warm-up patterns and activities on pages 12 to 29).
Reversals (writing letters and numerals back to front)	This is normal up until the age of about 8.	Use auditory and visual memory triggers; for example, tell your child that *b* looks a bit like a bat next to a ball. So for *b* say 'First the *bat* then the *ball*'.
Pencil grip and pressure	Correct grip (see page 9) is essential for relaxed and fluid writing.	Make sure pencils, paper or other writing surface is appropriate for your child's stage of development.
	Pencil tips that aren't broken	
Posture or body position	Correct positioning of wrist, arm, neck and shoulders, feet and paper is necessary to avoid pressure, hand cramps, discomfort or neck strain.	Sit correctly (check the PPP poster on page 112). Do warm-ups (see pages 12–29) and stretching.

Hungry panda

Help the panda find the bamboo.

Stay within the lines.

PARENT TIP: The maze requires your child to track between two lines to develop hand-eye coordination and fine motor control. Have your child do some big arm circles in the air to warm up before focusing on fine motor skills.

Bicycle race

Trace the lines.

Don't lift your pencil till the finish.

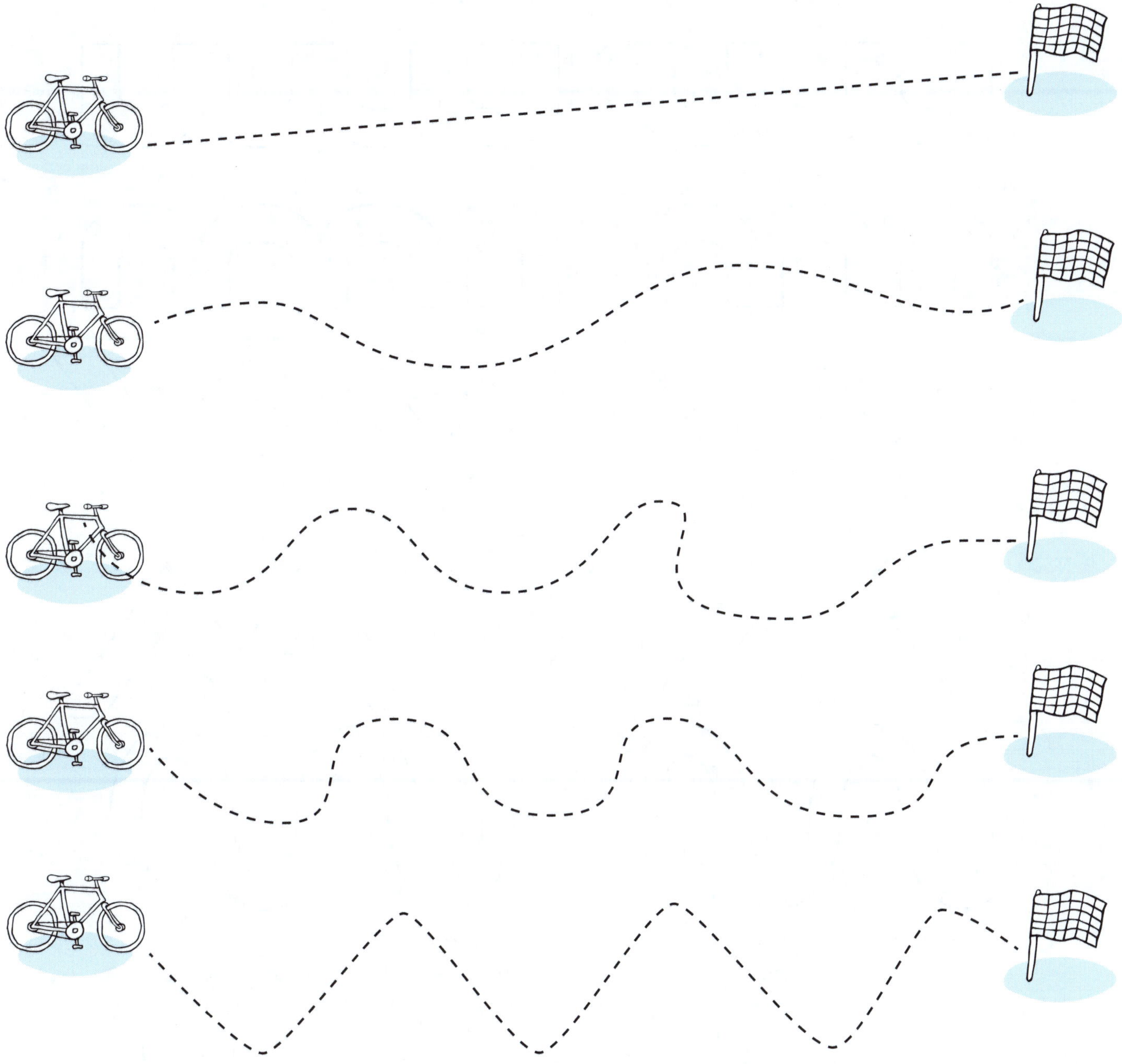

Which bicycle do you think will win the race? Circle it.

PARENT TIP: Tracing lines and patterns across the page helps reinforce the left-to-right direction of print. Tell your child to keep their pencil on the page the whole way across each line. Talk about the paths taken by each bicycle and which path is the most direct.

Tracking

Track within the shapes. Start at the dots.

Follow the arrows. Stay within the lines.

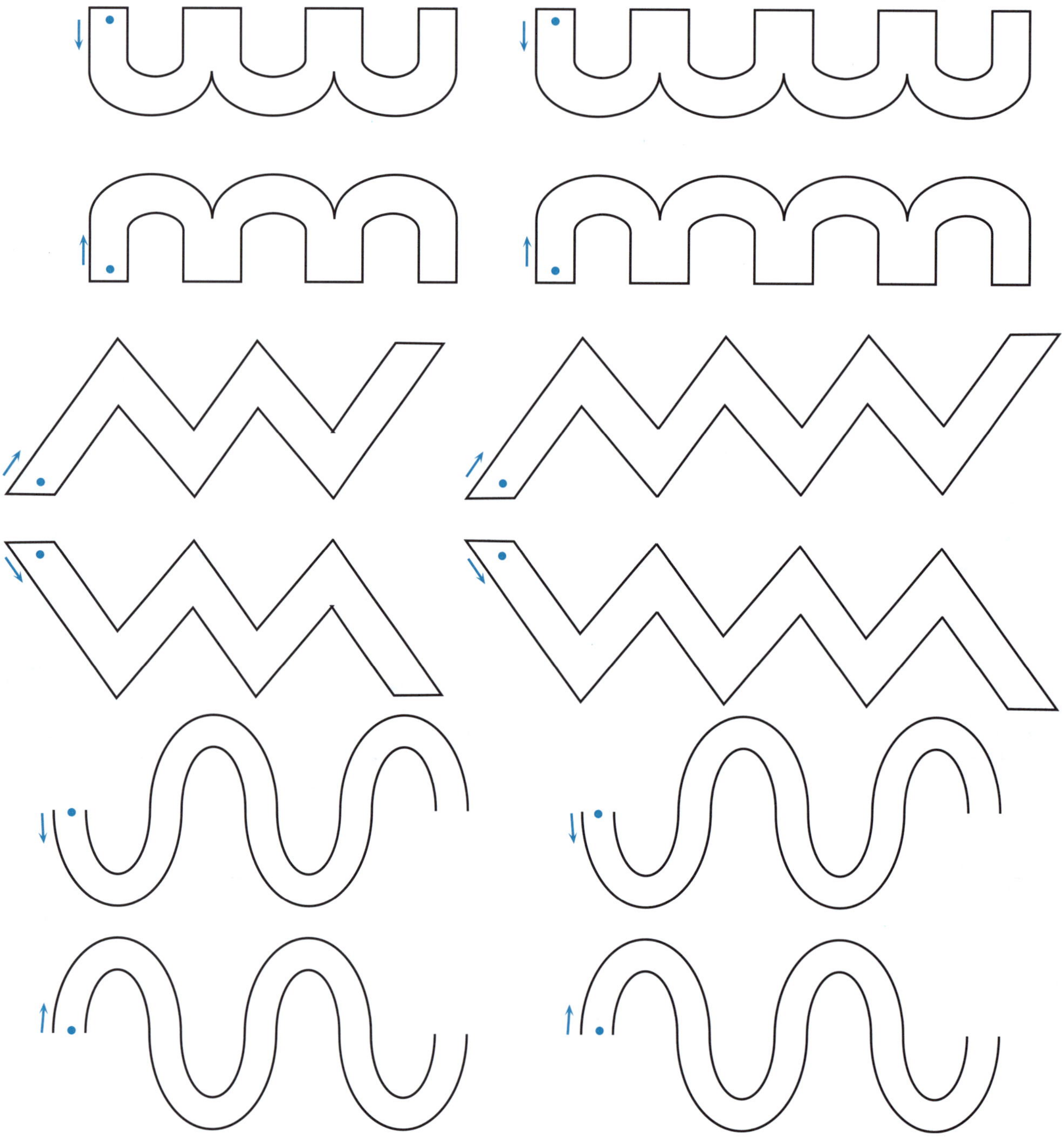

PARENT TIP: These tracking activities develop hand-eye coordination, fine motor control and muscle memory for handwriting movements and the direction of print.

Tracing

Trace the dotted lines. Neatly colour the animals.

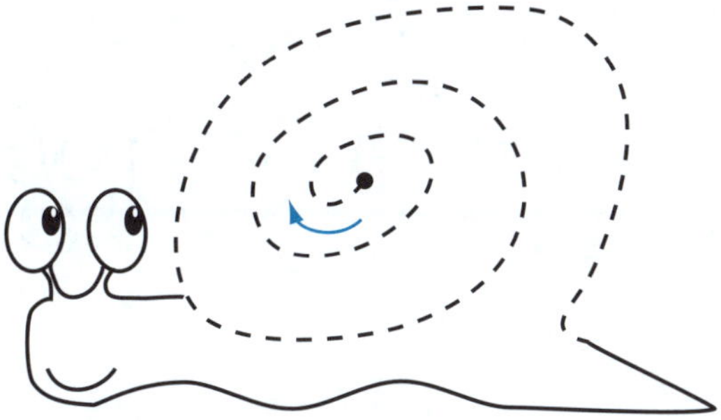

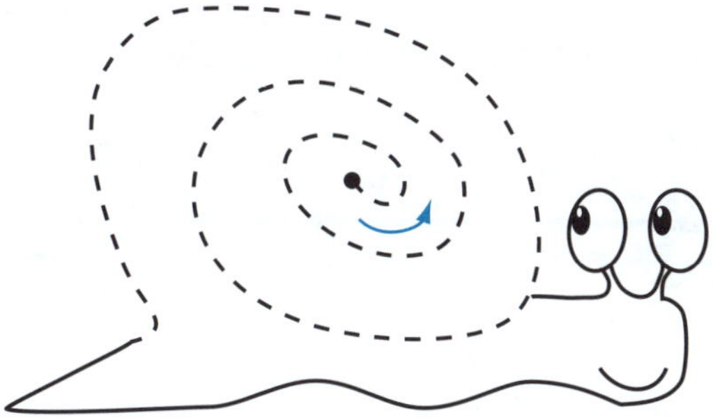

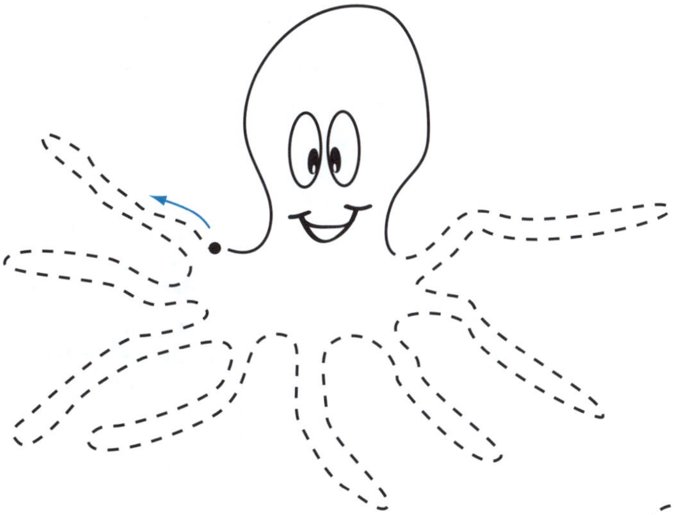

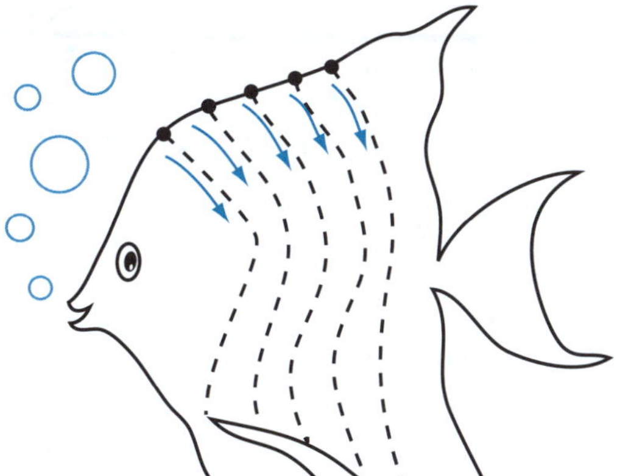

PARENT TIP: This activity helps develop fine motor control. Make sure your child starts at the start dots and follows the arrows, taking care to keep on the dotted lines. Have them colour the animals, staying within the lines. For a phonics activity, tell your child to listen for the first sound made when naming each animal (*s* in *snail*; *o* in *octopus*; *f* in *fish*; *p* in *peacock*). Then listen for other words that have the sounds.

Link the animals

Trace the dotted lines to link the pairs.

PARENT TIP: This activity supports development of fine motor control and hand-eye coordination. It also reinforces the left to right direction of print. Make sure your child does not lift the pencil until the end of each line.

Join the dots

Trace the first pattern on each line, then join the dots to copy the pattern across the line.

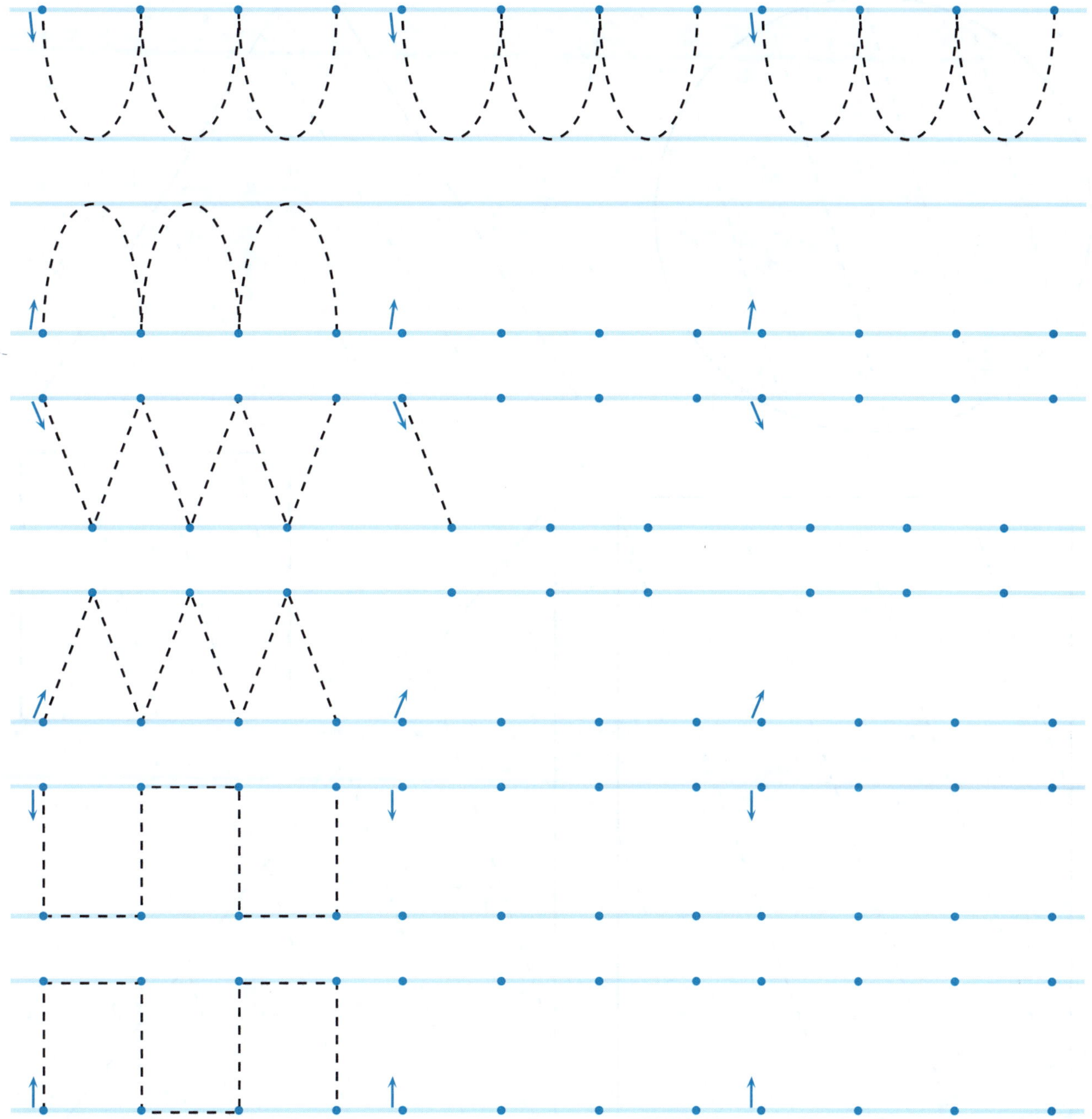

PARENT TIP: Patterns help children develop hand-eye coordination, fine motor control and visual discrimination. Watch that your child uses a relaxed and appropriate pencil grip. Activate both sides of your child's brain before they start by doing some cross-body activities: touch left hand to right shoulder, touch right elbow to left knee, and so on.

Shapes

Trace the lines within the shapes.

Start at the top and draw in a downwards direction.

PARENT TIP: On this page your child can practise the downstroke movement used in a number of letters and numerals. The downstrokes within each shape are sloped for the NSW Foundation Style of handwriting. The downstrokes are an equal distance apart and are parallel. Make sure your child traces the lines from the top down. Help your child learn the names of the shapes. Discuss aspects of each shape: How many sides? How many corners? Are the sides the same lengths?

Which one is the same?

Circle the shape on the right that is pointing the same way as the shape on the left.

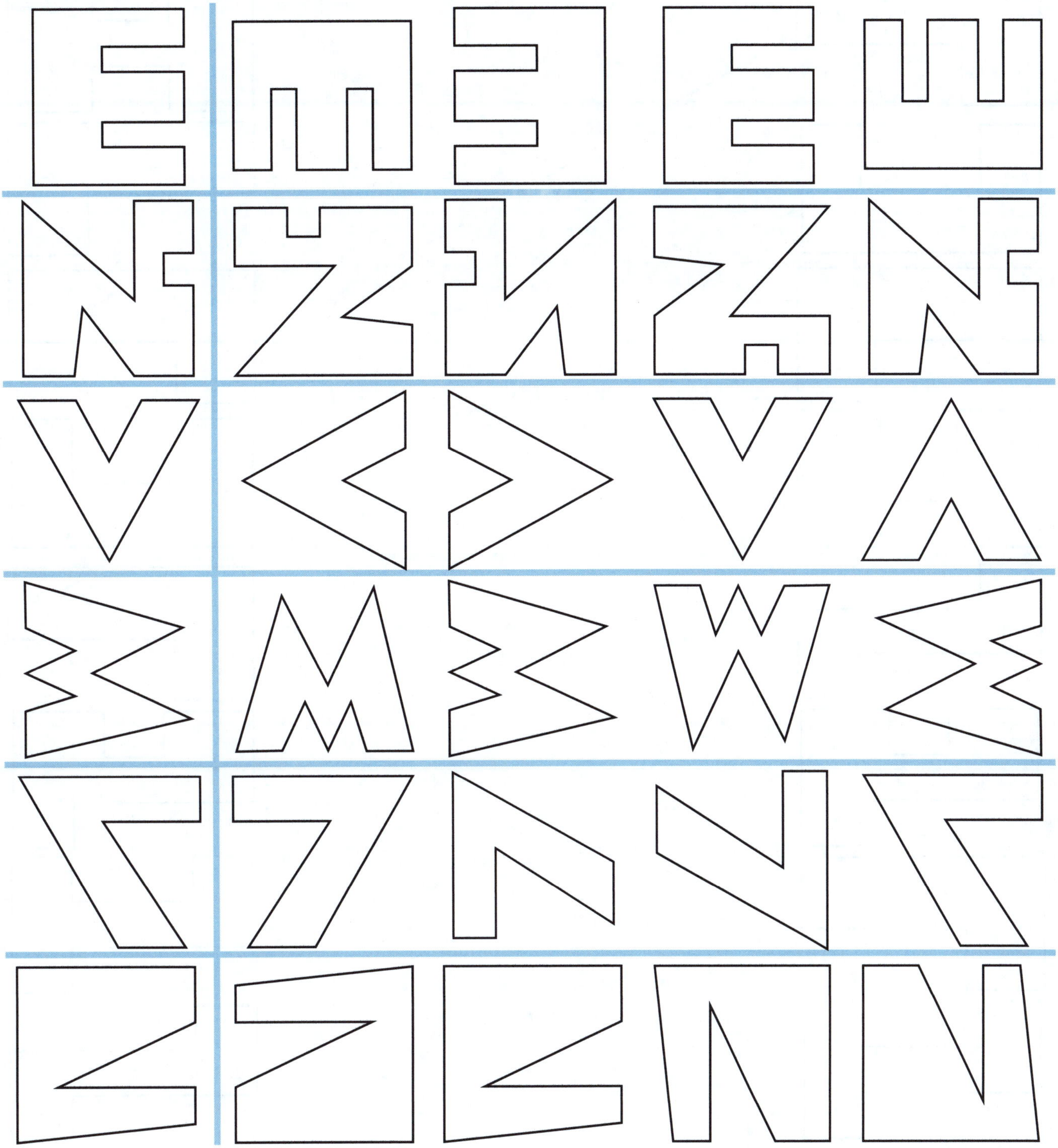

PARENT TIP: This is a visual discrimination activity. Children need this skill when they are learning letter shapes and how to differentiate between them. Make sure your child knows their left and right.

Link the matching shapes

Link each shape on the left to its matching shape on the right.

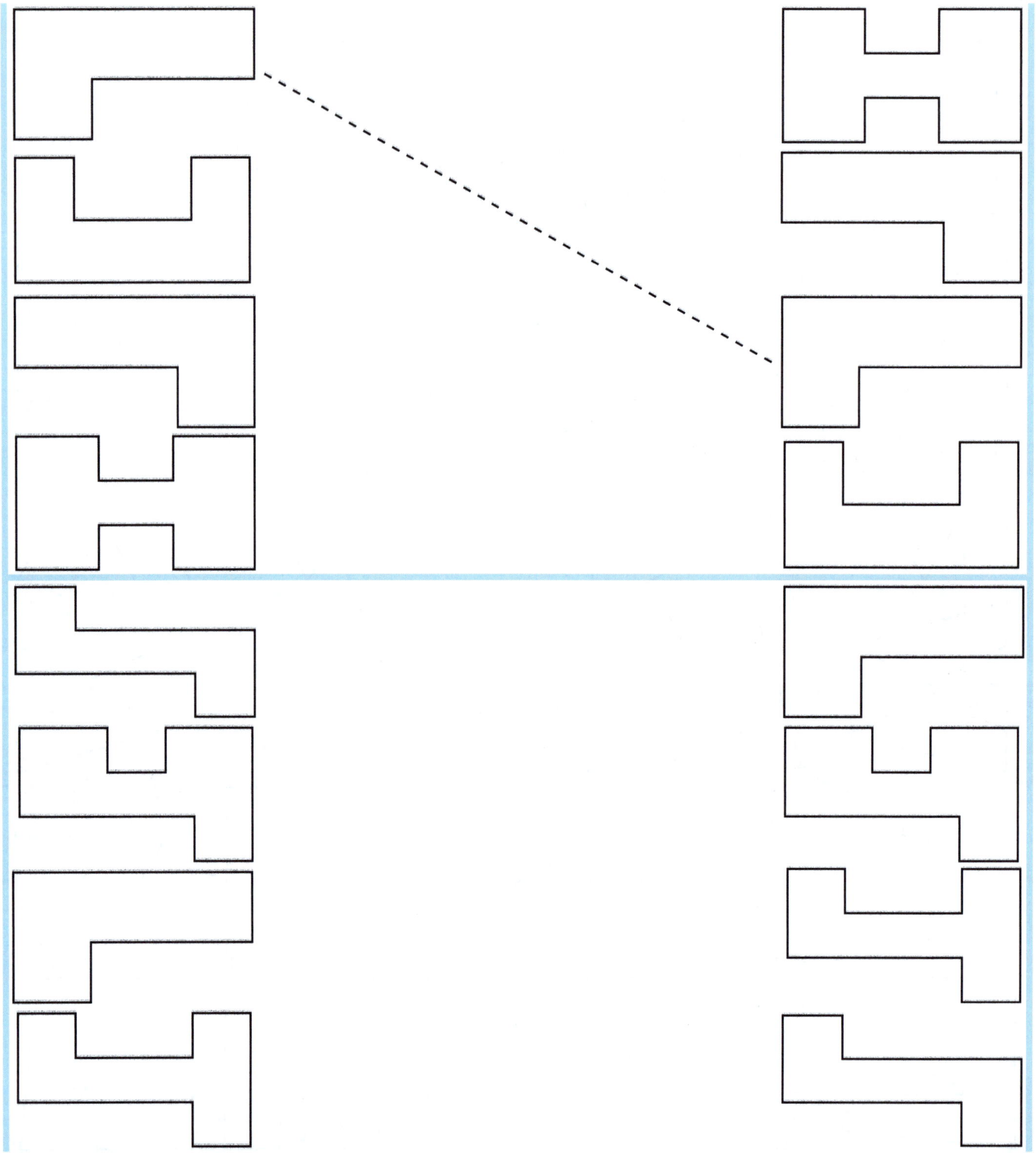

PARENT TIP: This is a visual discrimination activity. Children need this skill when learning to read and write so that they recognise letters in words and distinguish different words.

Straight lines

Trace each pattern. Then copy it across the line.

PARENT TIP: These patterns help your child to practise drawing straight lines and develop the downstroke movement. Ensure the strokes are parallel.

Clockwise patterns

Trace and continue each pattern.

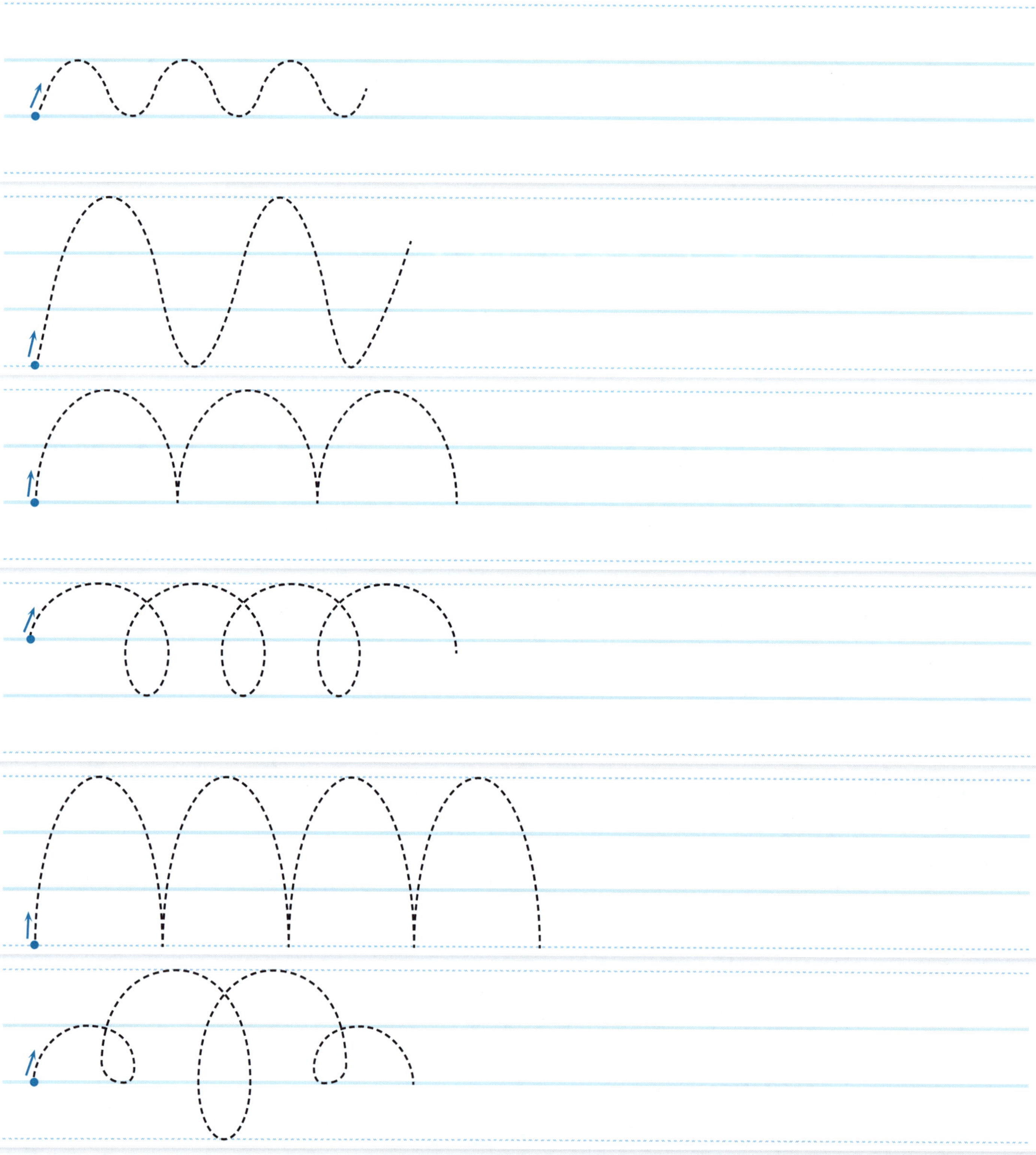

PARENT TIP: Have your child draw clockwise circles in the air to develop kinaesthetic memory for the movement. Have them practise the patterns on this page to develop hand-eye coordination and fine motor control for the clockwise movements required in numerous letters and numerals.

Anticlockwise patterns

Trace and continue each pattern.

PARENT TIP: Have your child draw anticlockwise circles in the air to develop kinaesthetic memory for the movements. Practising the patterns on the page helps children develop hand-eye coordination and fine motor control for the anticlockwise movement required in numerous letters and numerals. Practising with patterns supports the development of fluency in writing.

Find the hidden letter

Colour the puzzle pieces to find the hidden letter.

Colour G and g green. Colour Y and y yellow. Colour B and b blue.

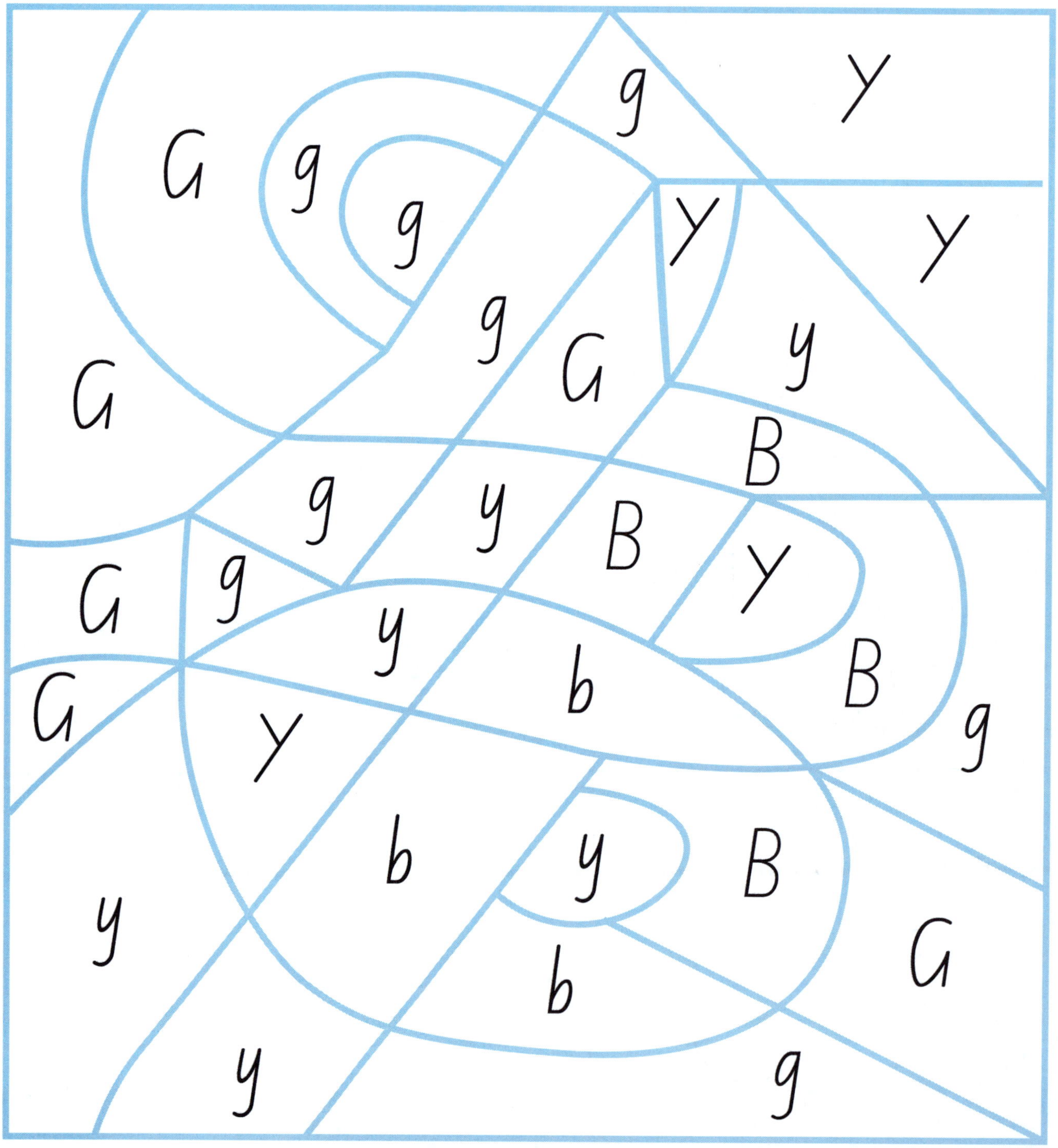

PARENT TIP: This is a visual discrimination activity. Students need to differentiate between the letter shapes. Children are also developing fine motor control when they colour in. The hidden letter is B.

Match the letters and numbers

Look at the letter/number patterns on the left.

Circle the matching letter patterns on the right.

5n	Sn nS 5m 5s 5n
vr	rv wv vr vn yr
hn	kn nh ln hn hm
Sz	5z Sz z5 Zx Sx
bd	db pq pd bp bd
ft	Fl tf lt ft ht

PARENT TIP: This is a visual discrimination activity. Children need this skill when learning to read and write so that they recognise letters in words and distinguish different words. Talk to your child about the shapes of the letters and which one comes first in the sequence.

Who's hiding?

Follow the numbers 1 to 10 to join the dots.

PARENT TIP: This activity helps children develop hand-eye coordination and fine motor control. It also reinforces counting to ten and number sequences to ten.

Matching more letters and numbers

Look at the letter patterns on the left.

Circle the matching letter patterns on the right.

da	ba ad ab da pa aq
pr	gr qr rp pr br rd
bo	ob bo db po do
lf	tf lt lf tl fl
3z	3n z3 n3 3z mS Sz
sz	zs xs kx wz sz

PARENT TIP: This is a visual discrimination activity. Children need this skill when learning to read and write so that they recognise letters in words and distinguish different words. Talk about the shapes of the letters and which one comes first in the sequence.

Join the dots

Copy the patterns.

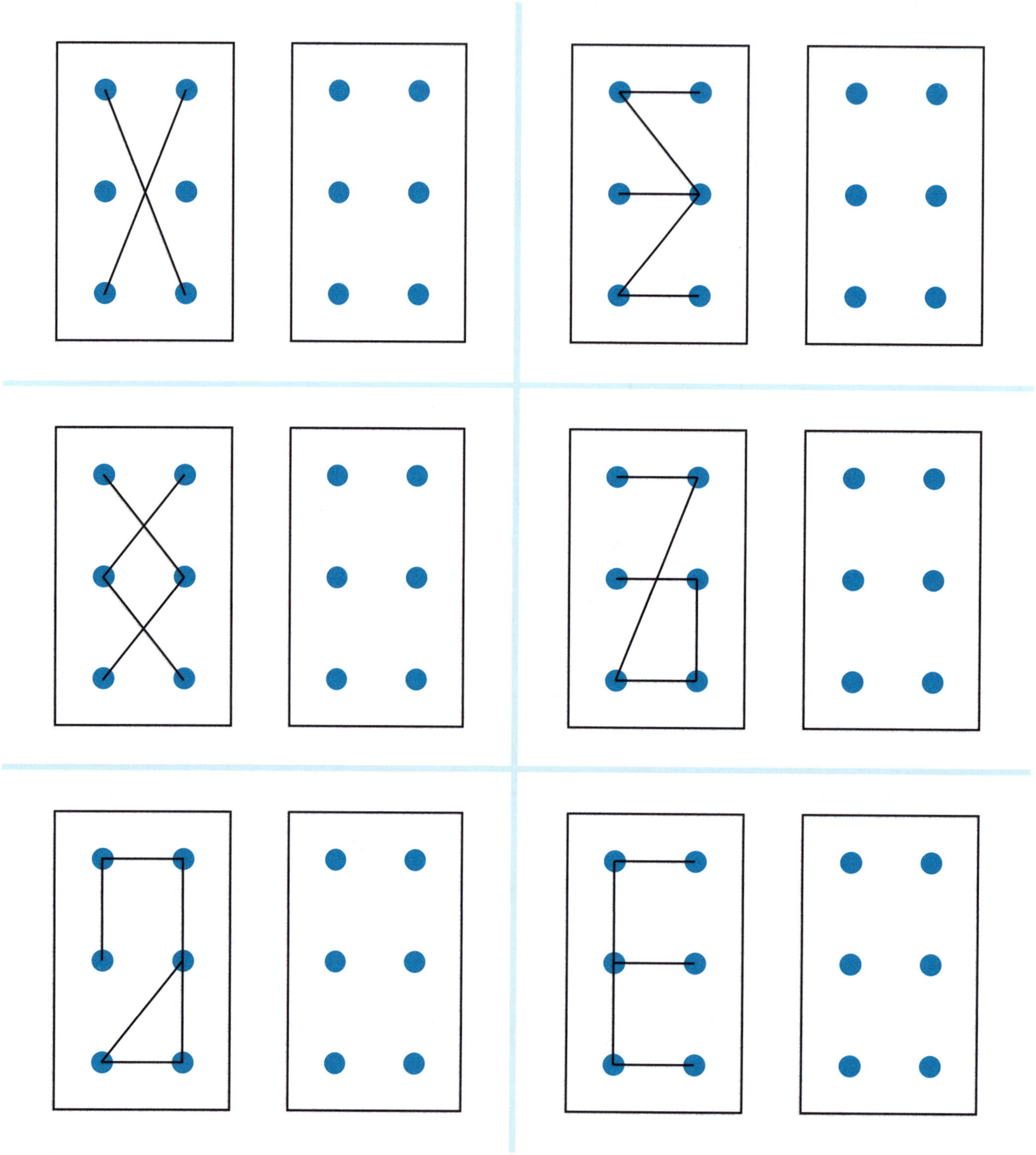

PARENT TIP: These patterns help children develop hand-eye coordination, visual discrimination and fine motor control.

Join more dots

Copy the patterns.

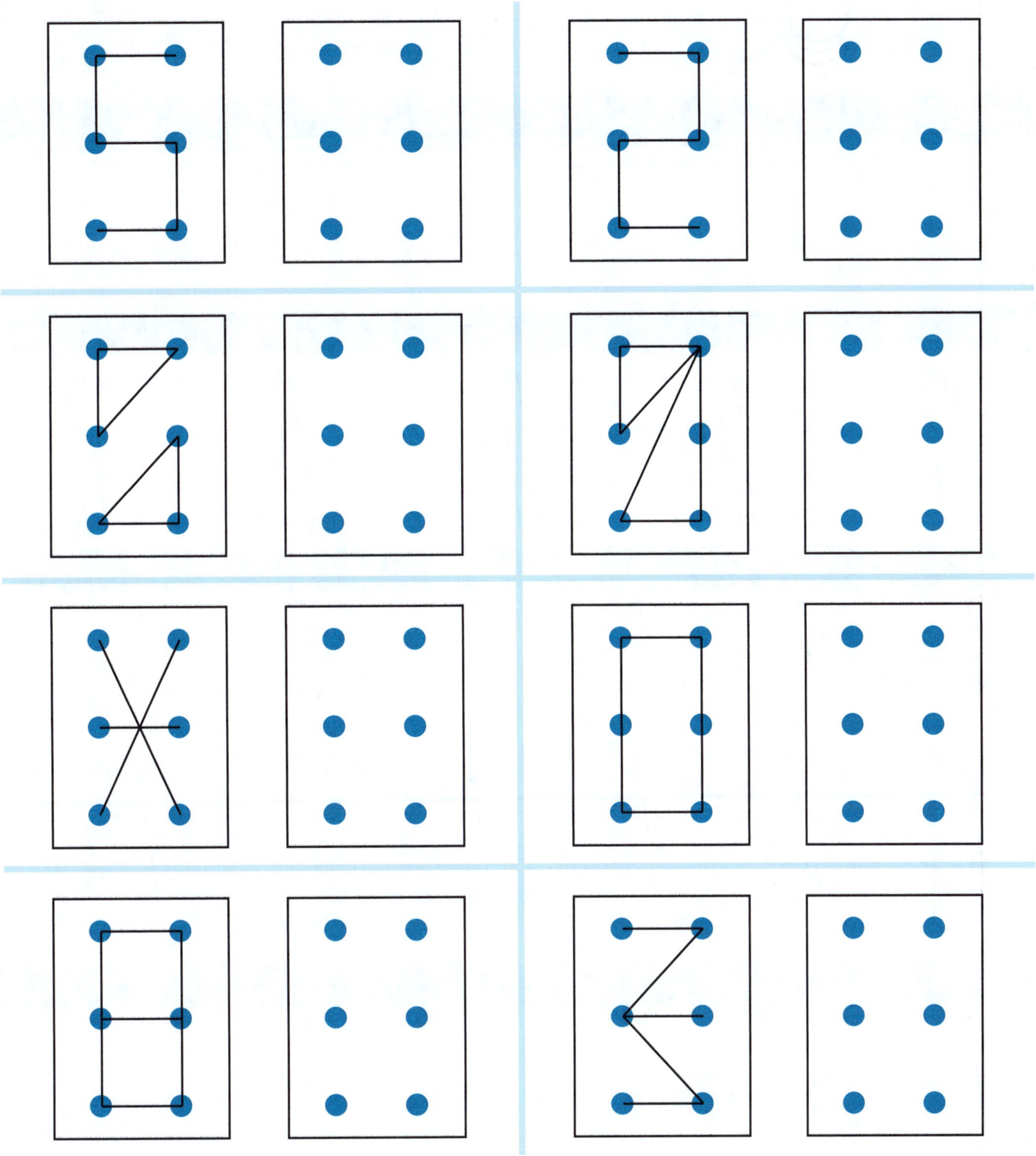

PARENT TIP: These patterns help children develop hand-eye coordination, visual discrimination and fine motor control.

Practice

Colour

Trace lamp

Track

Trace

Track

Trace

Try your own.

PARENT TIP: Before your child starts, have them check the Posture, Paper Tilt and Pencil Grip chart on page 112. Lower-case *l* is a tall letter. Point out to your child that it looks the same as the numeral one (*l*).

Practice

Colour

Trace

Lily

Track

L

Trace

Track

L L L L L

Trace

L

Try your own.

L

PARENT TIP: Point out the upper- and lower-case versions of the letter. Tell your child that a person's name always starts with the upper-case version.

Practice

Colour

Trace

truck

Track

Trace

Track

Trace

Try your own.

PARENT TIP: This is a tall letter. It requires your child to lift the pencil to cross the letter. The cross goes on the line. Check that your child crosses from left to right.

Practice

Colour

Trace

Tom

Track

Trace

Track

Trace

Try your own.

PARENT TIP: Point out that the upper-case version of this letter has the horizontal line at the top.

Practice

Colour

Trace

insect

Track

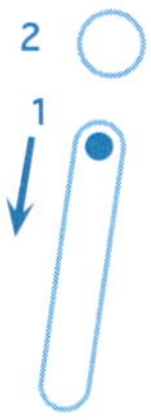

Trace

Track

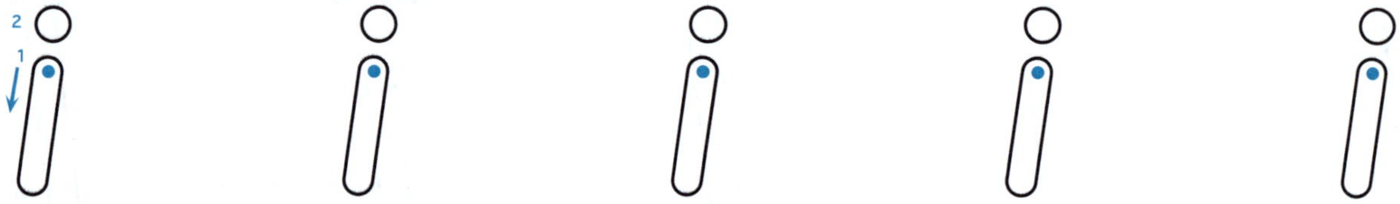

Trace

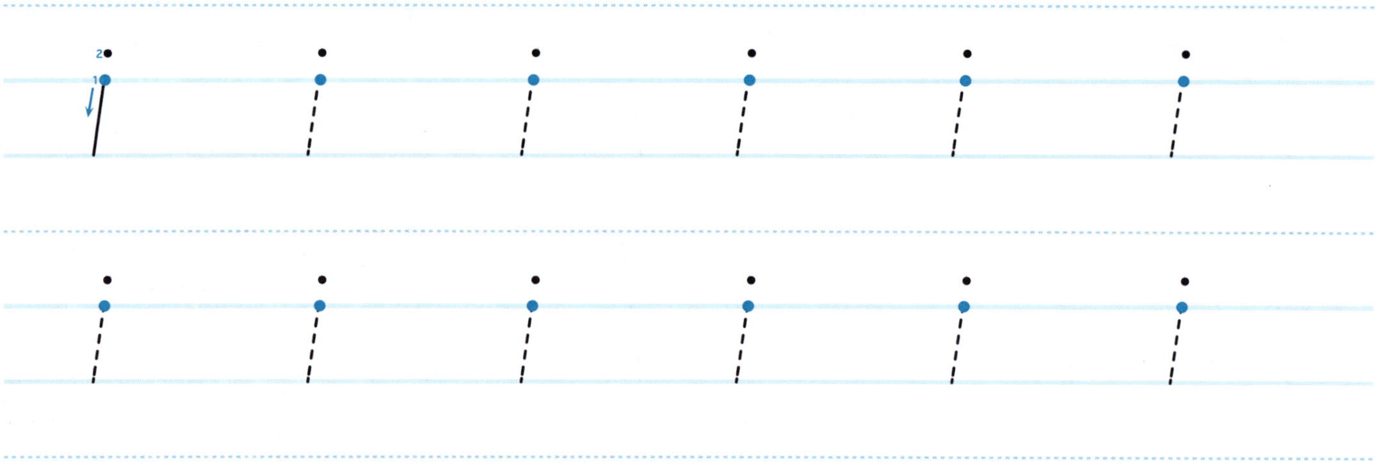

Try your own.

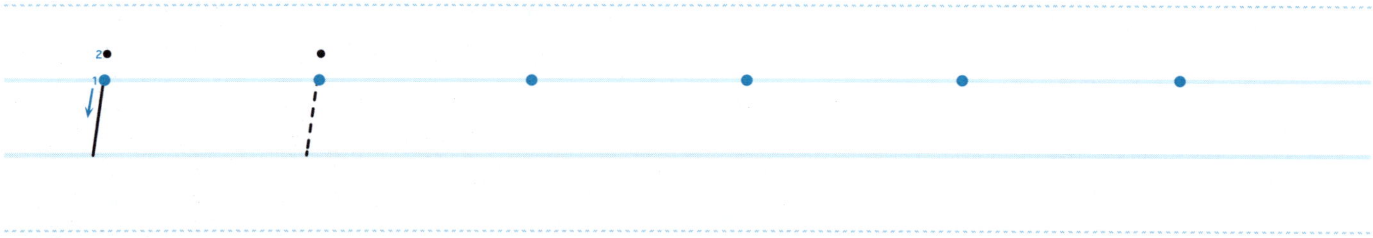

PARENT TIP: This letter requires your child to lift the pencil to dot the *i*. Repeat the sound of /i/ in insect. Ask your child to listen for the /i/ sound in these words: *in*, *it*, *tip*. Think of rhyming words for *tip*: *sip*, *zip*, *pip*, *hip*, *lip*, *dip*, *rip*, *kip*.

Practice

Colour

Trace

Isla

Track

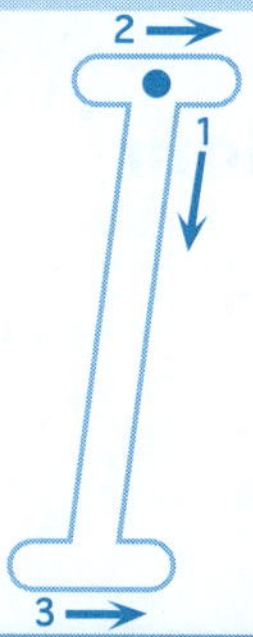

Trace

Track

Trace

2
1
3

Try your own.

2
1
3

PARENT TIP: Upper-case *I* is a tall letter. After the downstroke, your child will have to lift the pencil to put a horizontal line at the top and then lift the pencil again to put a horizontal line at the bottom. These two extra lines help avoid confusion with lower-case *l*.

Practice

Colour

Trace

fox

Track

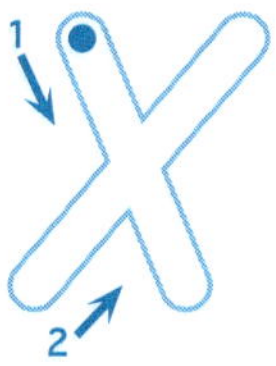

Trace

Track

Trace

Try your own.

PARENT TIP: Check that your child is using the non-writing hand to hold the page steady.

Practice

Colour

Trace Xander

Track X

Trace

Track

Trace

Try your own.

PARENT TIP: Upper-case X is the same as lower-case *x*, only bigger. Remind your child to start the first stroke at the top and the second stroke at the bottom, always moving from left to right.

Practice

Colour

Track

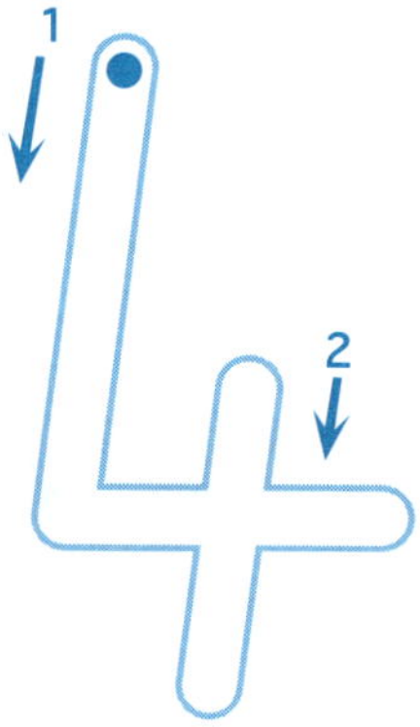

Track

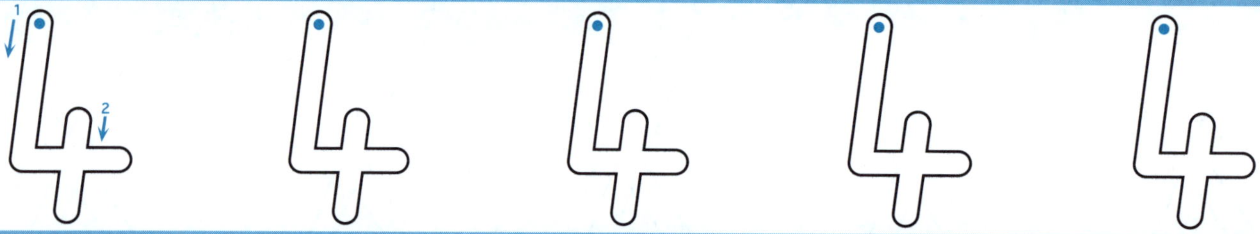

Trace

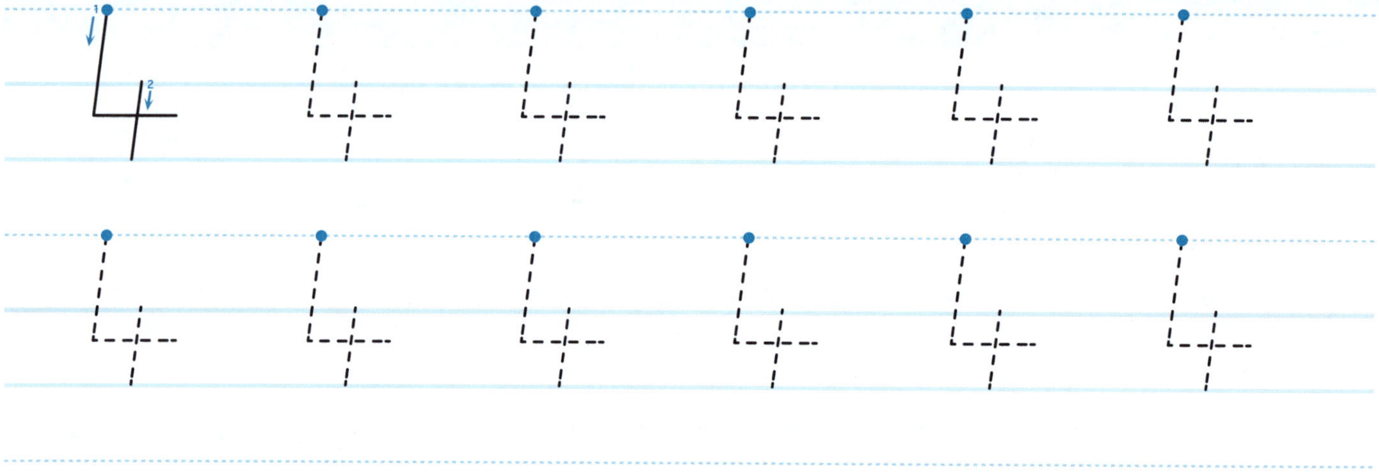

Try your own.

PARENT TIP: Your child will have to lift the pencil off the page for the second stroke. Watch that this second stroke is parallel to the first downstroke.

Revision

Track

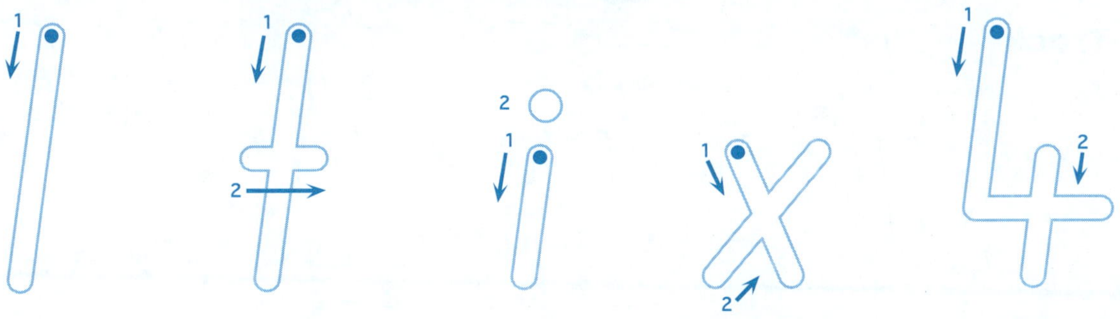

Trace, then try your own.

PARENT TIP: Remind your child when they need to lift the pencil for the dot (*i*) or for the second stroke (*t*, *x*, *4*).

Revision

Track

L T I X 4

Trace, then try your own.

L L L

T T T

I I I

X X X

4 4 4

PARENT TIP: Have your child do finger warm-ups and wrist circles before starting.

Practice

Colour

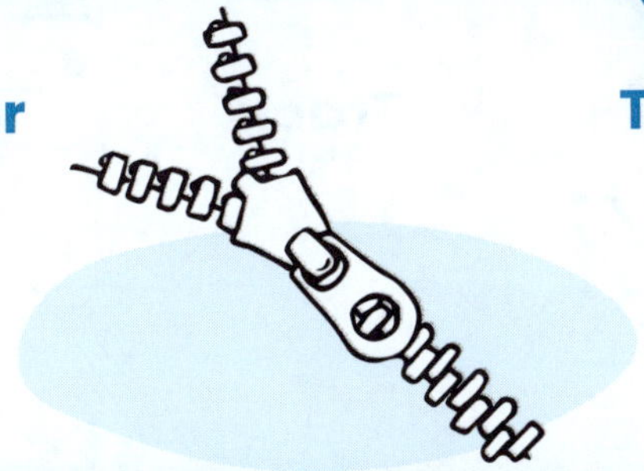

Trace

zipper

Track

1→ z

Trace

Track

Trace

Try your own.

PARENT TIP: Call this the zigzag letter. The letter starts at the top left. It moves to the right and from top to bottom without lifting the pencil off the paper.

Practice

Colour

Trace

Zara

Track

Trace

Track

Trace

Try your own.

PARENT TIP: The upper-case Z is the same as the lower-case version z only bigger. You could use the internet together to search for other names that begin with upper-case Z.

Practice

Colour

Trace

fish

Track

f

1

2

Trace

Track

1

2

Trace

1

2

Try your own.

1

2

PARENT TIP: This is a tall letter. The cross goes on the line, from left to right.

Practice

Colour

Trace

Finn

Track

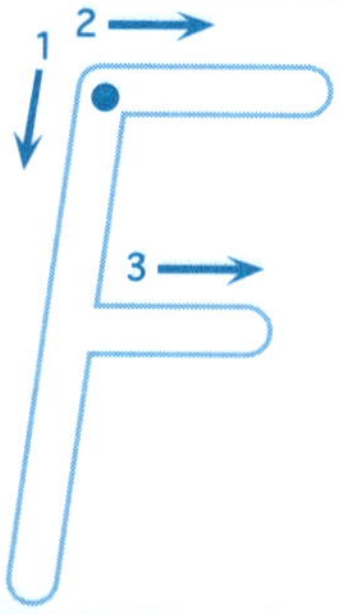

Trace

Track

Trace

Try your own.

PARENT TIP: Upper-case F has three strokes. Your child will need to lift the pencil twice. Make sure the two horizontal strokes are parallel.

Practice

Colour

Trace

jam

Track

2

1

j

Trace

Track

Trace

Try your own.

PARENT TIP: Your child can warm up by doing *jumping jacks* for *j*. Check that the tail or hook of the *j* reaches the lower line. Your child will need to lift the pencil to make the dot.

Practice

Colour

Trace

Jack

Track

Trace

Track

Trace

Try your own.

PARENT TIP: For upper-case J check that the tail or hook sits on the main line.

Practice

Colour

Track

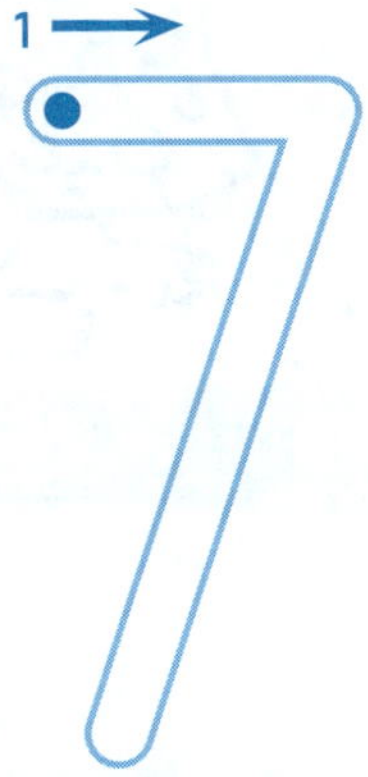

Track

Trace

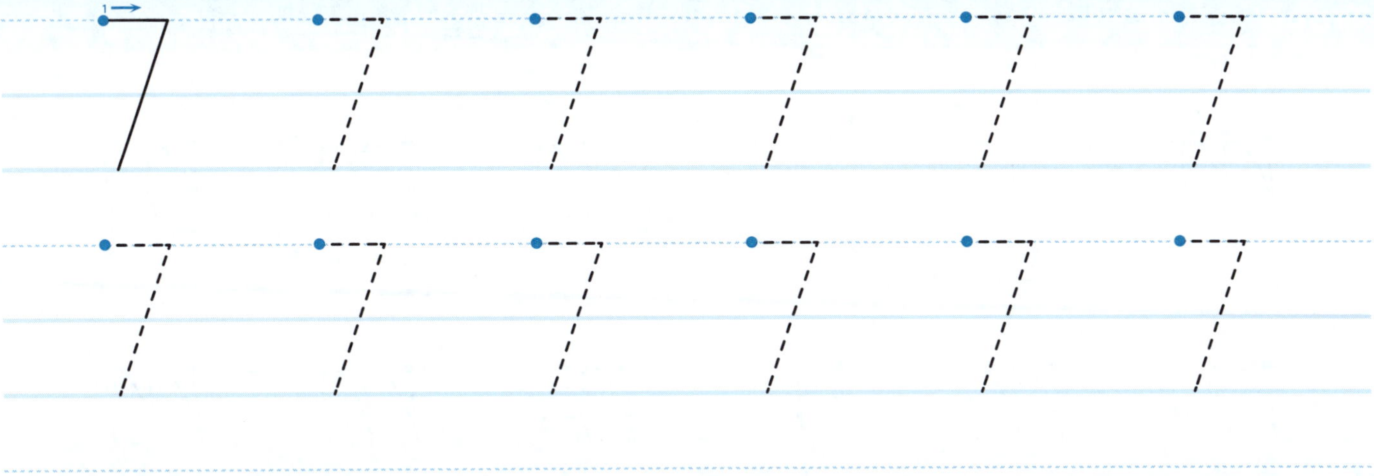

Try your own.

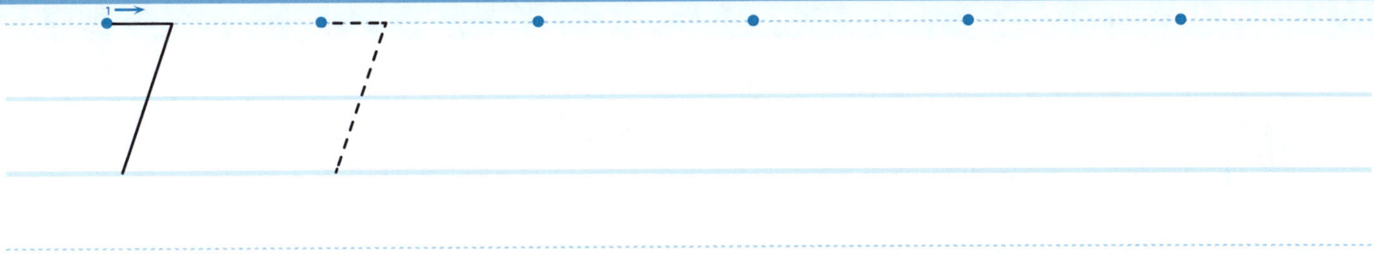

PARENT TIP: Do some stretching first: shoulders, arms, wrists and fingers. Point out that 7 starts at the top left, moves right and then moves down. This number is often reversed when children first start writing it.

Practice

Colour

Trace

mouse

Track

m

Trace

m m m

Track

m m m m m

Trace

m m m m m m

m m m m m m

Try your own.

m m

PARENT TIP: Lower-case *m* is like two round hills. Remind your child to start at the top left and go down first.

Practice

Colour

Trace Mia

Track M

Trace

Track

Trace

Try your own.

PARENT TIP: Upper-case M is like two pointy mountains. Your child will need to lift the pencil after the first downstroke.

Revision

Track

z f j 7 m

Trace, then try your own.

z z z

f f f

j j j

m m m

7 7 7

PARENT TIP: Lower-case *z* and the numeral *7* start the same way. Lower-case *f* and *j* have straight backs. Lower-case *m* is the letter that is made of two hills.

Revision

Track

Z F J 7 M

Trace, then try your own.

Z Z Z

F F F

J J J

7 7 7

M M M

PARENT TIP: Have your child pause during writing to do finger stretches and wrist circles. Shoulder circles are also useful to avoid back or neck strain.

Practice

Colour

Trace

net

Track

n

Trace

Track

n n n n n

Trace

n

Try your own.

n

PARENT TIP: Lower-case *n* is like one hill. Start at the top left to do the downstroke then trace back up and over for the hill.

Practice

Colour

Trace Noah

Track N

Trace

Track

N N N N N

Trace

N N N N N N

N N N N N N

Try your own.

N N

PARENT TIP: Check that your child starts at the top for the first downstroke. Your child will then need to lift the pencil. Watch that your child is applying the correct pressure with the pencil. Is the pencil pressing too heavily or lightly? Is the paper at risk of tearing? Is your child's wrist and arm relaxed or tense?

Practice

Colour

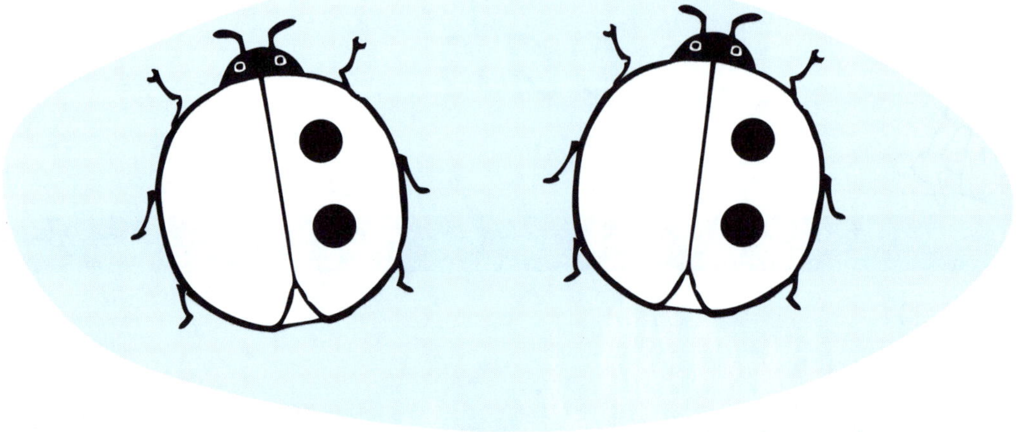

Track

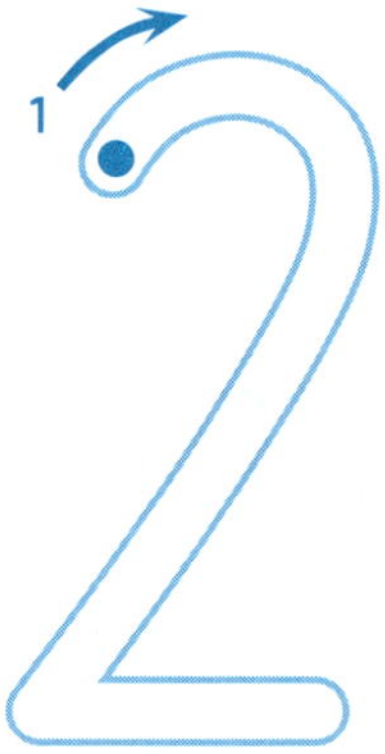

Track

Trace

Try your own.

PARENT TIP: This numeral often causes children problems. They often write it back-to-front. Check that your child makes one movement: begin with a clockwise curve, continue diagonally down to the main line, then make a left-to-right horizontal line.

Practice

Colour

Trace rabbit

Track r

Trace

Track

r r r r r

Trace

Try your own.

PARENT TIP: Remind your child to keep the pencil on the page for lower-case *r*. Move down, then trace back up to put the curve on the *r*.

Practice

Colour

Trace Remi

Track R

Trace

Track

R R R R R

Trace

R R R R R R

R R R R R R

Try your own.

R R

PARENT TIP: Make sure your child is sitting with the correct posture. Remind them to use the poster on page 112 to check for themselves. Brainstorm a list of people's names that begin with upper-case R.

Practice

Colour

Trace

hippo

Track

Trace

Track

Trace

Try your own.

PARENT TIP: The sound /h/ is like expelled air. Practise making the sound: /h/ /h/ /h/ then think of words that begin with the sound. The letter h is a tall letter. It starts at the top left with the downstroke and then moves back up and over to make a hill like n.

Practice

Colour

Trace Humza

Track

Trace

Track

Trace

Try your own.

PARENT TIP: Upper-case *H* has three movements so there are two pencil lifts. Ask your child to check that the two sides are equal and parallel.

Practice

Colour

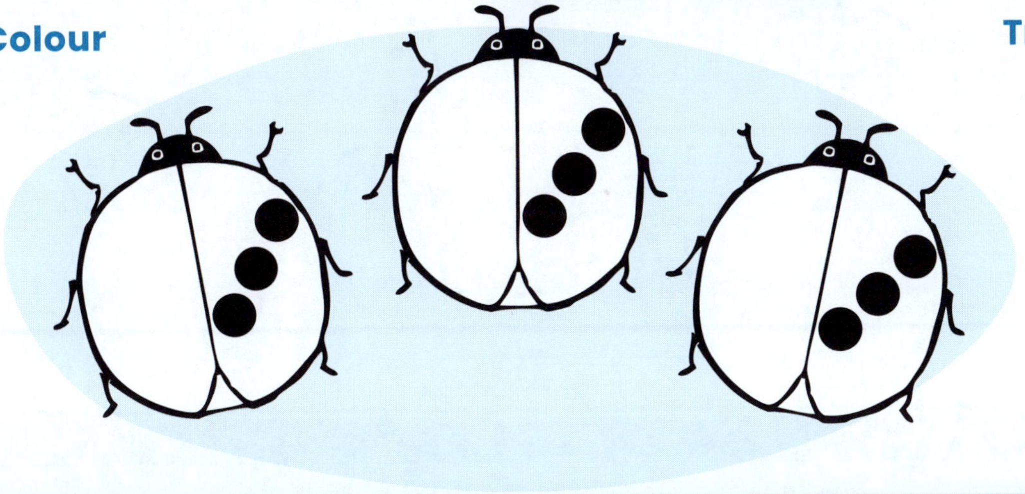

Track

Track

Trace

Try your own.

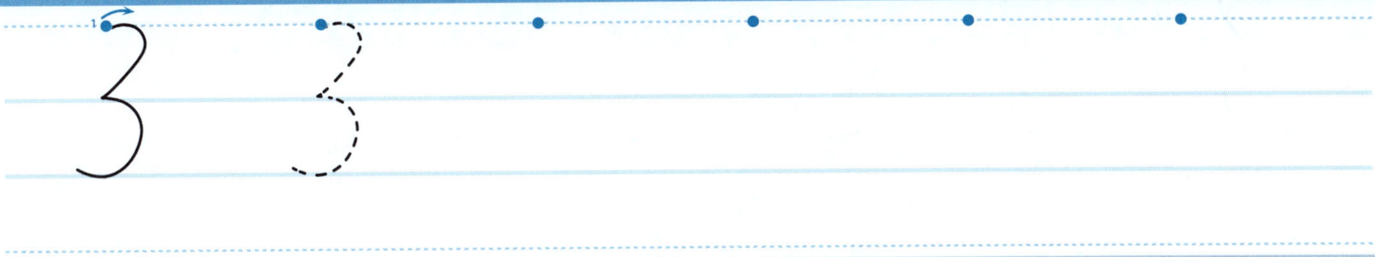

PARENT TIP: This numeral often causes children problems. Children often write it back-to-front. Remind your child that it is a clockwise numeral.

Revision

Track

n 2 r h 3

Trace, then try your own.

n n n

2 2 2

r r r

h h h

3 3 3

PARENT TIP: Remind your child that *2* and *3* start the same way, as clockwise curves. Remind them also that *r*, *n* and *h* all start with a downstroke and then trace back up.

Revision

Track

N 2 R H 3

Trace, then try your own.

N N N

2 2 2

R R R

H H H

3 3 3

PARENT TIP: Have your child circle their shoulders forwards and then backwards, then do some stretching. Cross-body movements are also useful to activate both sides of the brain.

Practice

Colour

Trace

bee

Track

b

Trace

Track

b b b b b

Trace

b

Try your own.

b

PARENT TIP: Lowercase *b* and *d* often confuse children. Help your child to remember *b* by pointing out it looks a bit like a bat next to a ball and saying 'First the *bat* and then the *ball*'. Both words start with *b*.

Practice

Colour

Trace

Bayo

Track

B

Trace

Track

Trace

Try your own.

PARENT TIP: Your child has to lift the pencil after the downstroke. The two clockwise curves are made with one movement.

Practice

Colour

Trace

panda

Track

p

Trace

Track

p p p p p

Trace

p p p p p p

p p p p p p

Try your own.

p p

PARENT TIP: Lower-case *p* and *b* can be confusing. Check that the bottom of the letter *p* reaches the lower line and that your child is writing *p* without lifting the pencil. Remind your child of the bat and ball memory trigger for *b* to differentiate from *p*. *P* sounds like a *puff*. Think of words that begin with the sound: *pip*, *pup*, *pop*, *pat*, *pet*, *pot*, *pit*.

Practice

Colour

Trace

Paige

Track

Trace

Track

Trace

Try your own.

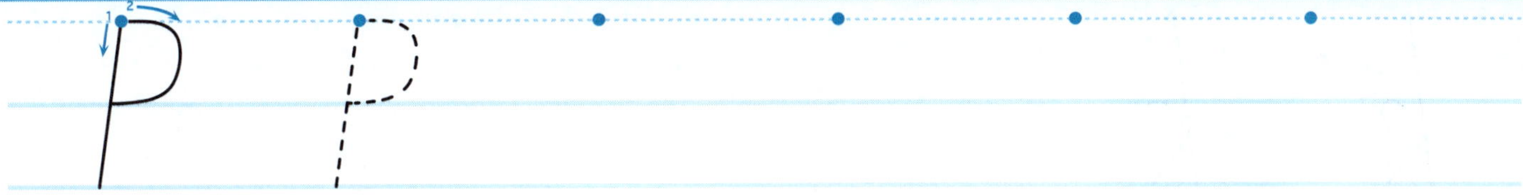

PARENT TIP: Check that your child has a relaxed grip and posture when writing so that writing does not cause neck or wrist strain.

Practice

Colour

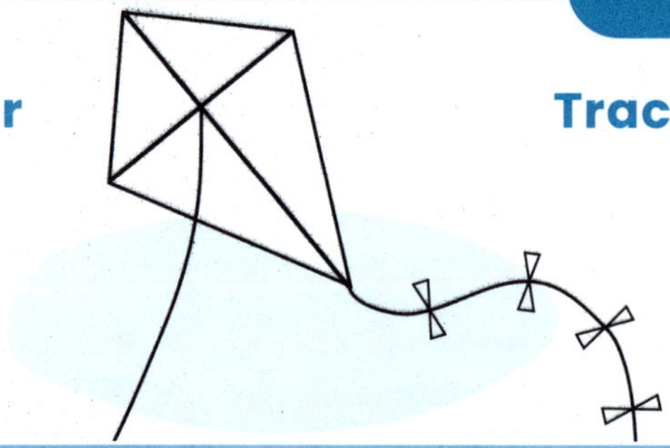

Trace

kite

Track

k

Trace

Track

k k k k k

Trace

k k k k k k

k k k k k k

Try your own.

k k

PARENT TIP: Lower-case *k* is made without lifting the pencil off the page.

Practice

Colour

Trace Kai

Track K

Trace

Track

K K K K K

Trace

K

Try your own.

K

PARENT TIP: Uppercase K has two movements so one pencil lift is needed.

Practice

Colour

Track

Track

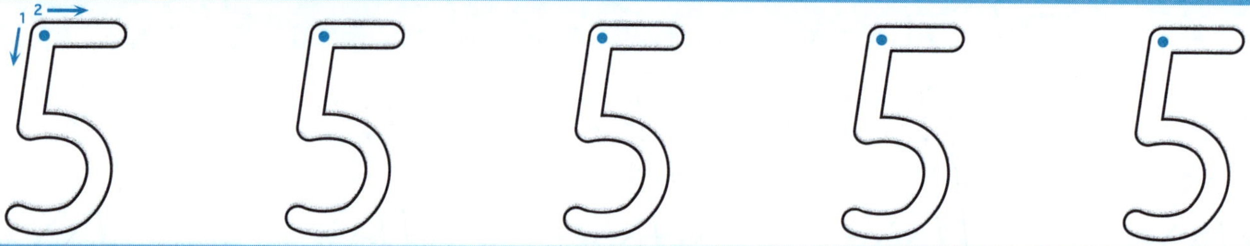

Trace

Try your own.

PARENT TIP: The numeral *5* can be tricky to write. It has straight lines and a clockwise curve. It is a commonly reversed letter. It will need a pencil lift to finish with a horizontal stroke at the top. Practice makes perfect.

Practice

Colour

Trace umbrella

Track u

Trace

Track

Trace

Try your own.

PARENT TIP: Lower-case *u* is similar to a smiley mouth with a downstroke to finish.

Colour

Trace Una

Track U

Trace

Track

Trace

Try your own.

PARENT TIP: Upper-case U is the same as lower-case *u*, only taller.

Revision

Track

b p k 5 u

Trace, then try your own.

b b b

u u u

k k k

5 5 5

p p p

PARENT TIP: This revision page mixes clockwise and anticlockwise movements so remind your child about the movements. Have your child do some warm-ups for the movements on spare paper before starting the page.

Revision

Track

B P K 5 u

Trace, then try your own.

B B B

P P P

K K K

5 5 5

u u u

PARENT TIP: Have your child do some cross-body warm-ups to activate the left and right hemispheres of their brain. For example, touch right hand to left shoulder and left elbow to right knee. Have them do wrist twirls and finger warm-ups.

Practice

Colour

Trace

volcano

Track

v

Trace

Track

Trace

Try your own.

PARENT TIP: Make the sound for /v/ with your child. Think of words beginning with the /v/ sound; for example, *vet*, *van*, *visit*, *vase*, *violin*.

Practice

Colour

Trace Violet

Track V

Trace

Track

Trace

Try your own.

PARENT TIP: Upper-case V has a pointy bottom. It looks like a cone.

Practice

Colour

Trace

wombat

Track

w

Trace

Track

Trace

Try your own.

PARENT TIP: Lower-case *w* is like two waves. The word *waves* also begins with a *w*.

Practice

Colour

Trace

Wen

Track

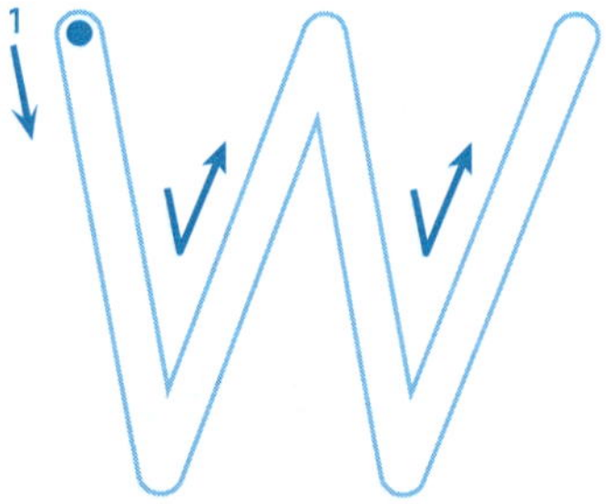

Trace

Track

Trace

Try your own.

PARENT TIP: Upper-case W is like two cones with pointy bottoms.

Practice

Colour

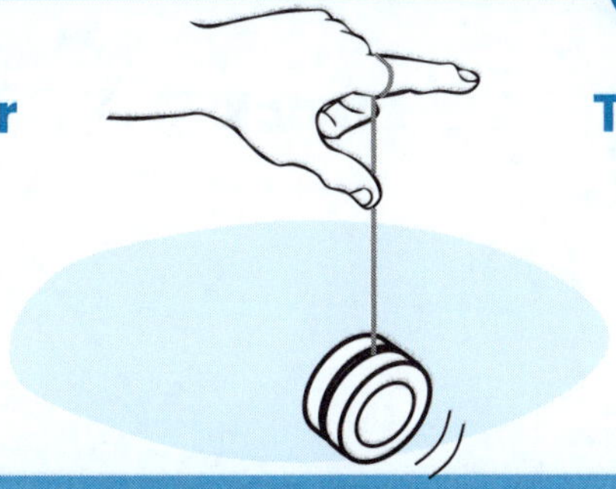

Trace

yo-yo

Track

y

Trace

Track

y y y y y

Trace

y y y y y y

y y y y y y

Try your own.

y y

PARENT TIP: This letter begins as a letter *u* and ends with a tail that curves backwards on the lower line.

Practice

Colour

Trace Yoshi

Track y

Trace

Track

Trace

Try your own.

PARENT TIP: Have your child check the Posture, Paper Tilt and Pencil Grip poster on page 112 to self-correct if they need to. Are they up-to-date on the progress tracker on page 4?

Practice

Colour

Trace

ant

Track

a

Trace

Track

a a a a a

Trace

a a a a a a

a a a a a a

Try your own.

a a

PARENT TIP: Lower-case *a* moves anticlockwise and ends with a downstroke. The body is not a circle—it is elliptical.

Practice

Colour

Trace

Ava

Track

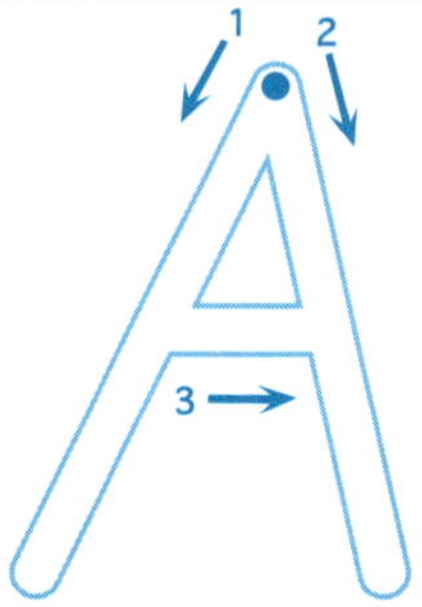

Trace

Track

Trace

Try your own.

PARENT TIP: Upper-case *A* needs two pencil lifts. Point out that the name *Ava* contain both an upper-case *A* and a lower-case *a*.

Practice

Colour

Trace

cat

Track

c

Trace

Track

Trace

Try your own.

PARENT TIP: This letter uses an anticlockwise movement. Help your child think of words that begin with this sound. Some will be *k* words (*kite*, *kookaburra*, *kitchen*, *koala*). Write the words and explain that two letters can make the same sound at times. Help your child segment the individual sounds in words.

Practice

Colour

Trace Clem

Track C

Trace

Track

Trace

Try your own.

PARENT TIP: Upper-case C is the same as lower-case c, only taller.

Revision

Track

v w y a c

Trace, then try your own.

v v v

w w w

y y y

a a a

c c c

PARENT TIP: Remind your child that the letters v, w and y begin in a similar way. The letters a and c begin the same way as each other, moving in an anticlockwise direction.

Revision

Track

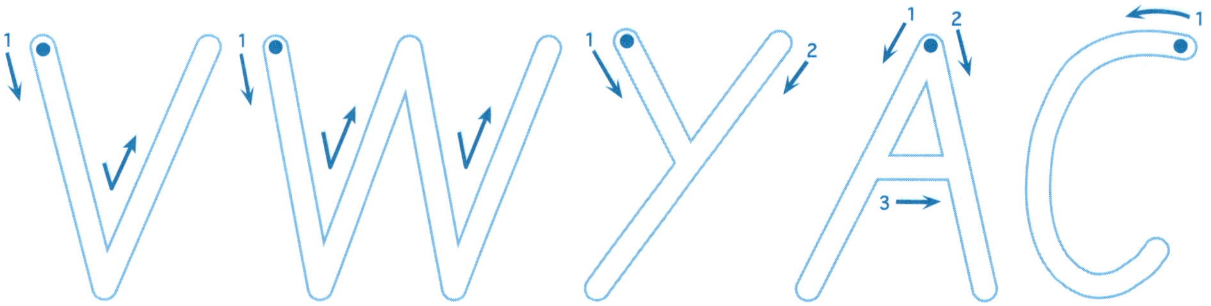

Trace, then try your own.

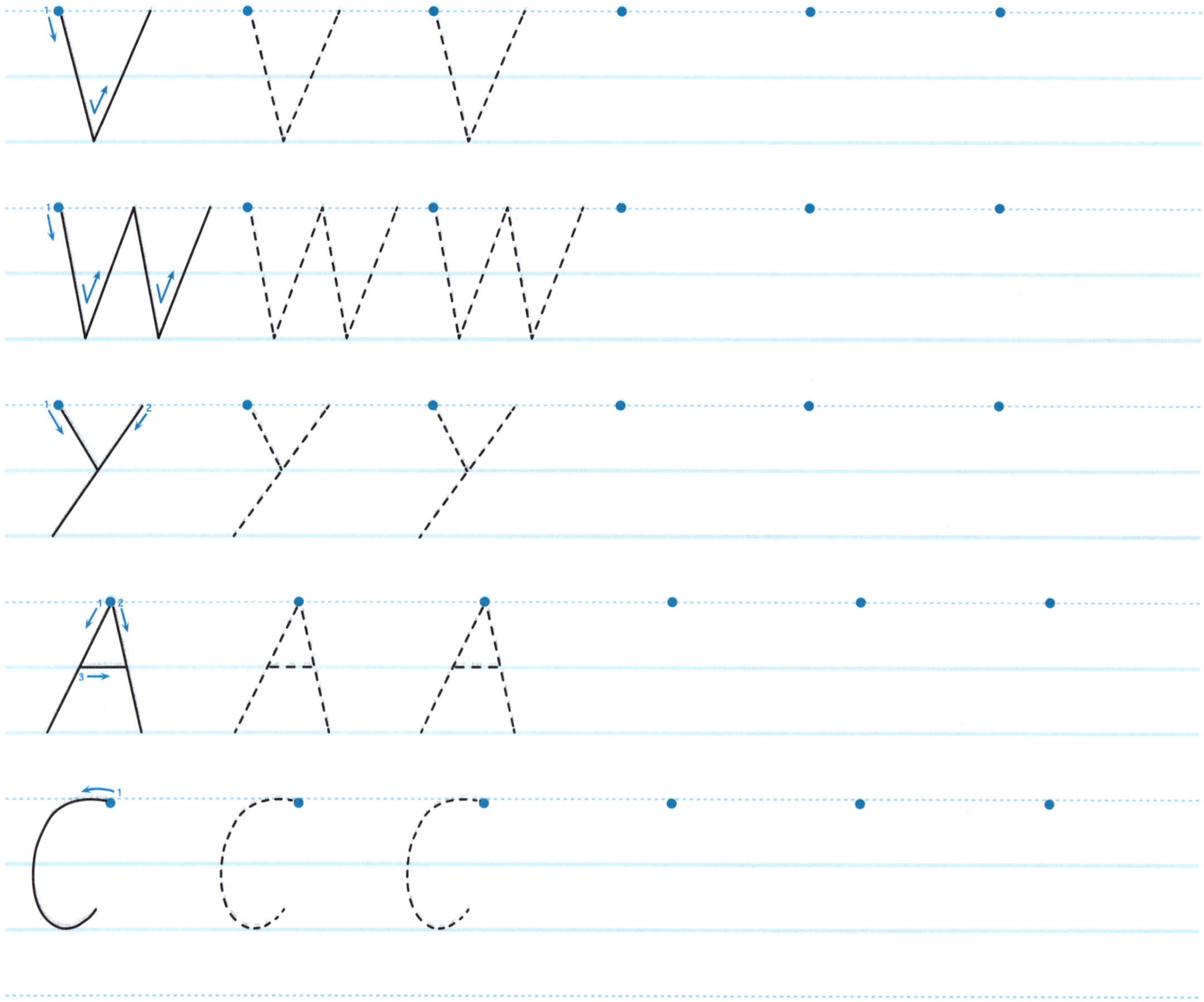

PARENT TIP: Ask your child to reflect on their writing progress. Look back to the beginning of the book or any pages done earlier if working out of page sequence. Can your child see an improvement? Has your child been doing other fine motor control activities if extra attention is needed for this?

Practice

Colour

Track

Track

Trace

Try your own.

PARENT TIP: The numeral 6 is made with one movement. Try big arm movements in the air first.

Practice

Colour

Trace

ox

Track

Trace

Track

Trace

Try your own.

PARENT TIP: This is an elliptical letter. It is written in an anticlockwise direction. Your child can hear its sound in *pop*, *top*, *hot*, *rot*, *not*, *dot*, *mop*. Make a list of words with this sound and read them with your child.

Practice

Colour

Trace

Oliver

Track

Trace

Track

Trace

Try your own.

PARENT TIP: This letter is an ellipse, not a circle. Remind your child not to grip the pencil too tightly. Relax the writing hand.

Practice

Colour

Track

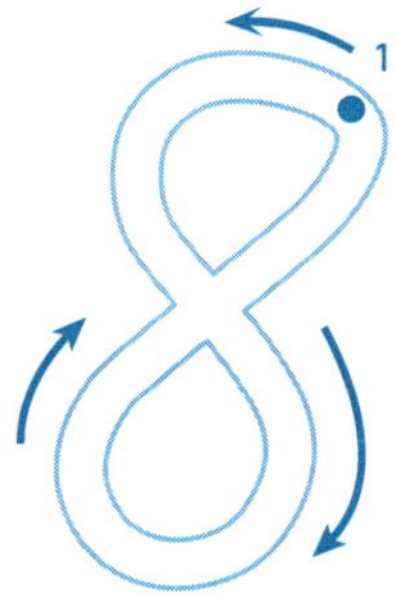

Track

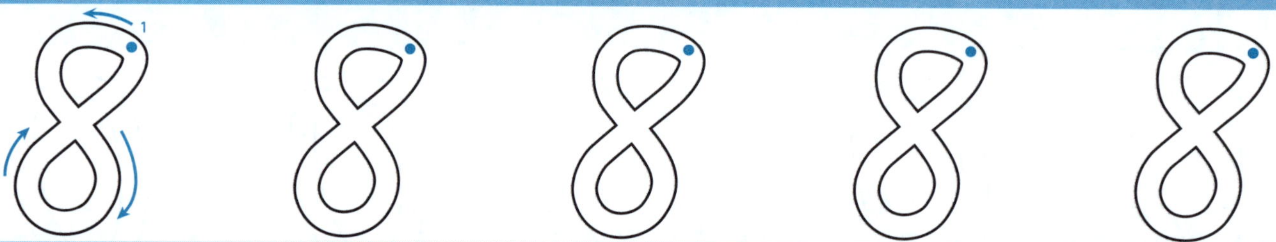

Trace

Try your own.

PARENT TIP: This numeral is made without lifting the pencil. Have your child use big arm movements to make the numeral in the air before writing on paper.

Practice

Colour

Trace

guitar

Track

Trace

Track

Trace

Try your own.

PARENT TIP: Make the hard /g/ sound for your child, as in: *guitar, girl, got, get, goat*. Check that when they write the letter *g*, the tail reaches down to the lower line.

Practice

Colour

Trace Georgia

Track G

Trace

Track

G G G G G

Trace

G

Try your own.

G

PARENT TIP: Brainstorm all the names you and your child can think of that begin with upper-case *G*: *George*, *Gina*, *Gail*, *Gabrielle*, *Gabby*, *Gabriella*, *Gracie*, *Gino*, etc. Note that *G* can make a hard sound as in *Gail* or a soft sound as in *Gino*.

Practice

Colour

Trace

queen

Track

Trace

Track

Trace

Try your own.

PARENT TIP: This letter has a tail with a slight flick on the bottom. It is made with one movement. Check that your child does not lift the pencil.

Practice

Colour

Trace Quinn

Track

Trace

Track

Trace

Try your own.

PARENT TIP: Lift the pencil to add the flick at the bottom in a left-to-right direction.

Revision

Track

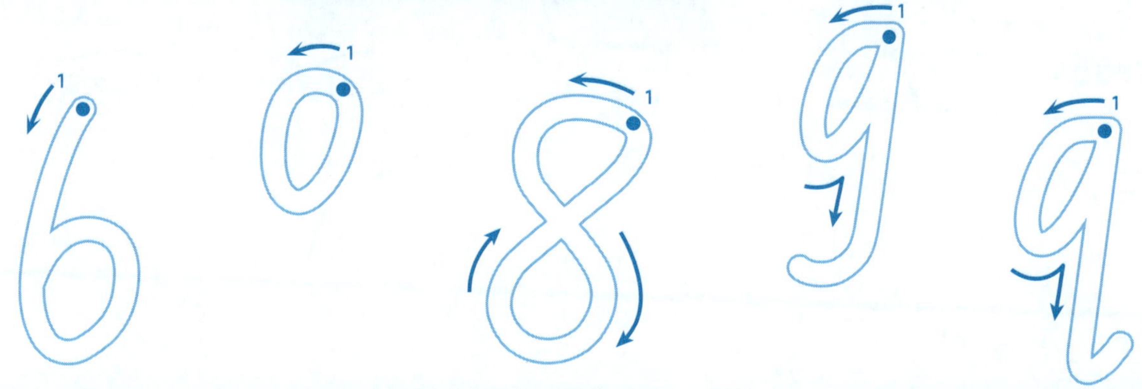

Trace, then try your own.

PARENT TIP: All these revision letters and numerals start with anticlockwise movement. Practise in the air with big arm movements before writing. Remind your child not to confuse lower-case g and q. Their tails go in opposite directions.

Revision

Track

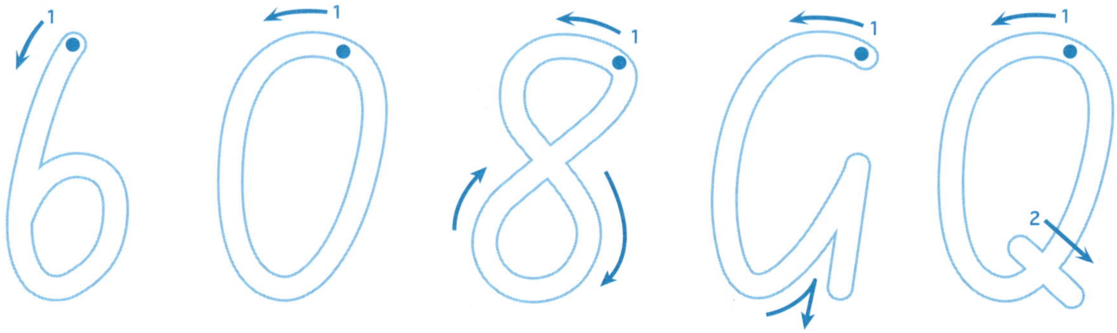

Trace, then try your own.

PARENT TIP: Each of these revision letters and numerals begins with an anticlockwise movement.

Practice

Colour

Track

Track

Trace

Try your own.

PARENT TIP: The numeral 9 looks like the lower-case q, without the flick of the tail.

Practice

Colour

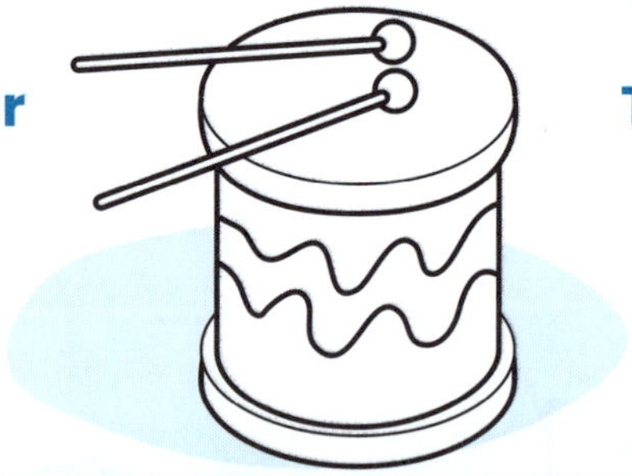

Trace

drum

Track

d

Trace

Track

Trace

Try your own.

PARENT TIP: Lower-case *b* and *d* confuse many children. Use the memory trigger of the word *bed*. If your child can remember the shape of this word and the /*b*/ and /*d*/ sounds, it might help them distinguish *b* from *d* when they write.

Practice

Colour

Trace Dabir

Track

Trace

Track

Trace

Try your own.

PARENT TIP: Tell your child that names of places begin with upper-case letters. Look on an atlas or a map to find places beginning with upper-case *D*.

Practice

Colour

Trace elf

Track e

Trace

Track

Trace

Try your own.

PARENT TIP: Lower-case *e* starts in the middle of the letter. Lower-case *d* is the only other letter that starts in the middle.

Practice

Colour

Trace

Emma

Track

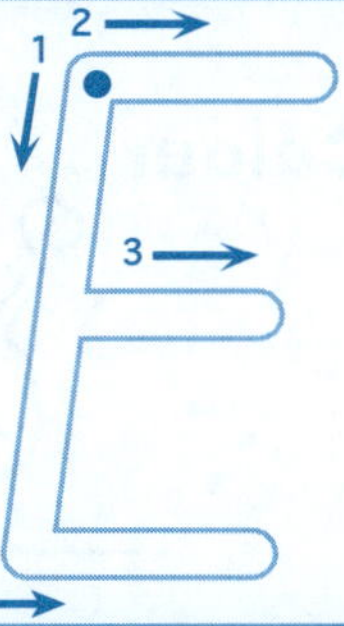

Trace

Track

Trace

Try your own.

PARENT TIP: Upper-case *E* begins with an *L*. Then add the top and middle horizontal strokes.

Practice

Colour

Trace

snail

Track

s

Trace

Track

s s s s s

Trace

s s s s s s

s s s s s s

Try your own.

s s

PARENT TIP: s is the snake letter. It makes a hissing sound. It's an easy letter for children to remember but its curves need practising.

Practice

Colour

Trace

Saeed

Track

Trace

Track

Trace

Try your own.

PARENT TIP: Make up silly animal names that begin with upper-case *S*; for example, *Sally the salamander*, *Snippy the snake.*

Practice

Colour

Track

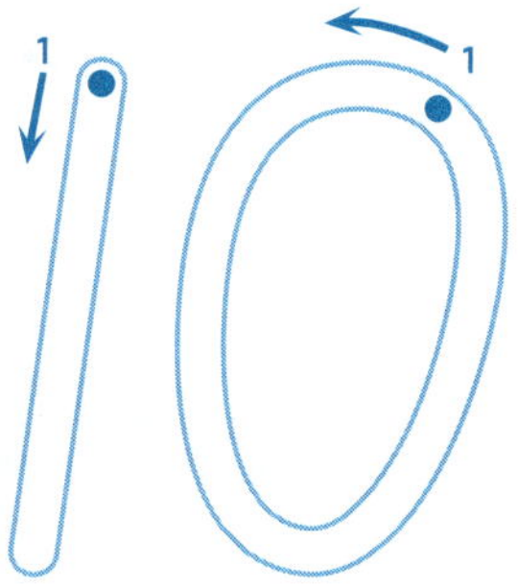

Track

Trace

Try your own.

PARENT TIP: Check the elliptical shape of the 0.

Revision

Track

q d e s 10

Trace, then try your own.

q q q

d d d

e e e

s s s

10 10 10

PARENT TIP: These letters and numbers all use anticlockwise movements. Practise the movements in the air or on scrap paper.

Revision

Track

9 D E S 10

Trace, then try your own.

PARENT TIP: This revision page includes a mix of anticlockwise (9, S, 0), clockwise (D) and downstroke (l, E) movements. Your child will need to concentrate on starting each letter and numeral correctly.

Writing words

Trace the words.

the the the the the

of of of of of of

and and and and and

to to to to to to to

in in in in in in in

is is is is is is is

Writing words

Trace the words.

you you you you you

that that that that

it it it it it it it it

he he he he he he

was was was was

for for for for for

Writing words

Trace the words.

on on on on on on

are are are are are

as as as as as as

with with with with

his his his his his

they they they they

My own words

Write your own words on the lines.
These can be words you know or words you'd like to learn.

NSW Foundation Style

a b c d e f g

h i j k l m n

o p q r s t u

v w x y z

0 1 2 3 4 5

6 7 8 9 10

NSW Foundation Style

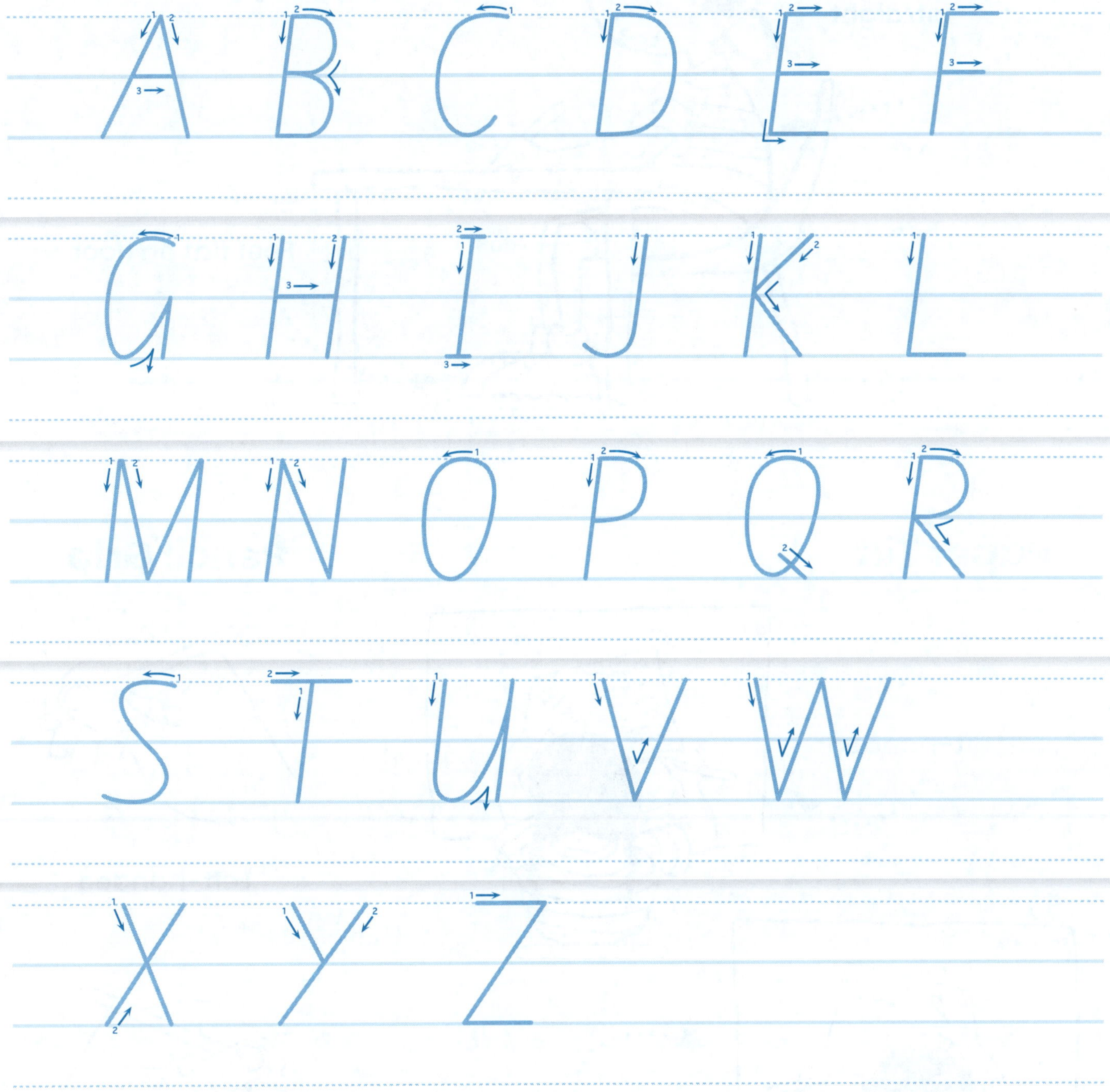

Posture, paper tilt and pencil grip

Posture

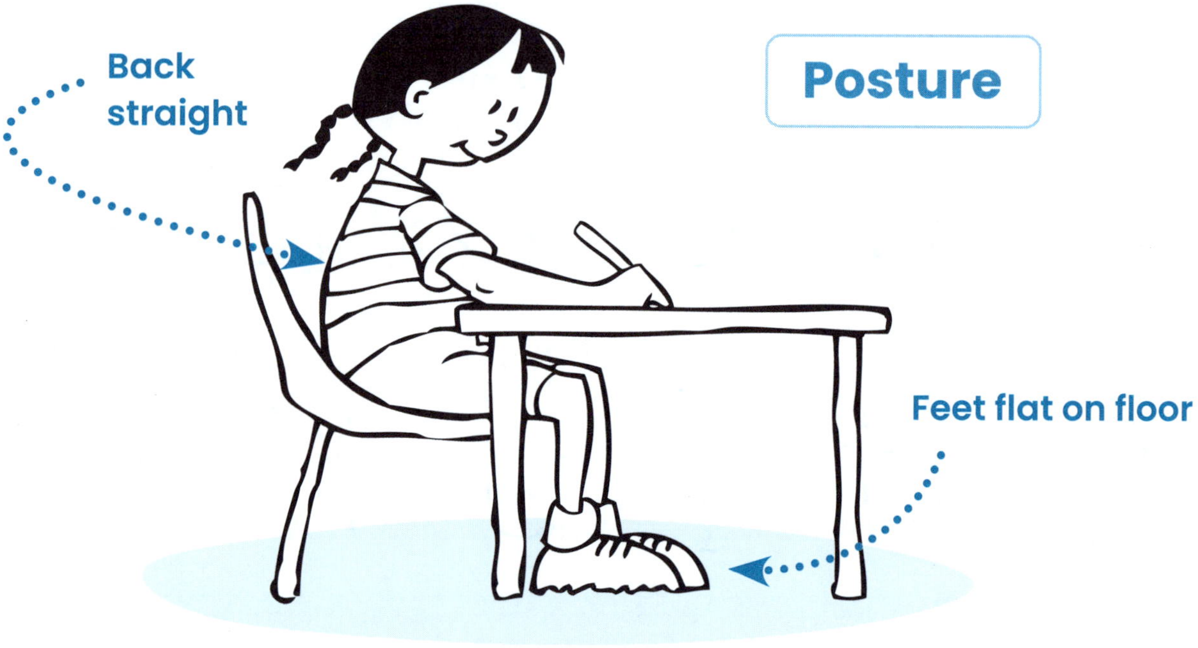

Paper Tilt

Pencil Grip

Left-handed

Right-handed